CREATING BACK SCENES

FOR MODEL RAILWAYS AND DIORAMAS

DAVID WRIGHT

THE CROWOOD PRESS

First published in 2017 by
The Crowood Press Ltd
Ramsbury, Marlborough
Wiltshire SN8 2HR

www.crowood.com

British Library Cataloguing-in-Publication Data
A catalogue record for this book is available from the British Library.

ISBN 978 1 78500 280 9

DEDICATION AND SPECIAL THANKS

I would like to dedicate this, my fifth book, to my late brother Dennis and the Macmillan Cancer Support team at the Derbyshire Royal Infirmary (now The Royal Derby Hospital), and thank them for their dedication in his final weeks. My eldest brother took me on many trips out around the country as a young boy to experience the rich and diverse landscape of the British Isles. It was these early encounters, especially walks in the Peak District of Derbyshire, that inspired most of the landscape modelling and back scene painting presented in the pages of this book.

Also I would like to pass on my special thanks to: Clive Baker, Phil Waterfield, Martin Nield, Dave Richards, Tim Jeffcoat, Colour Rail, Andy York (of *BRM*) and the Mickleover Model Railway Group for their valuable contributions towards producing this book.

Typeset by Shane O'Dwyer, Swindon, Wiltshire

Printed and bound in Malaysia by Times Offset (M) Sdn Bld

CREATING
BACK SCENES

FOR MODEL RAILWAYS AND DIORAMAS

CONTENTS

INTRODUCTION

My interest in model railways was re-kindled over twenty-five years ago. In this time, I have seen a host of model railway layouts at exhibitions and model railway clubs. They have been built to all the modelling scales and depicted many different periods of the British railway scene, and a good number have represented scenes away from British shores.

The standard of the layouts has for the most part been very high, especially with regard to the locomotives and rolling stock. Some even go as far as operating the layout to a prototypical timetable. I have, however, often been a little disappointed when it comes to the scenic elements, particularly in terms of the back scene that has been provided, or, in some cases, the complete lack of a back scene. Surely, if a modeller is prepared to go to great lengths to replicate detail

and achieve realism on certain areas of the layout, this should be carried through to the scenics and especially the back scene. There is nothing worse, especially at the exhibitions, than seeing unsightly equipment and the belongings of a layout operator lying behind the layout in full view of the public.

Anyone attempting to build a model railway will need to try their hand at a number of different skills; in fact, it is this aspect that makes the hobby so diverse. No one can be expected to be a master of every craft involved, but it is worth having a go, and can lead to great satisfaction. Many modellers instinctively claim to be 'no artist' when it comes to creating a back scene, and may wonder why they should bother when pre-printed back scenes are easily available from model suppliers. I hope to change the minds

The perfect image of a steam train set in the British landscape. The rural background of the Pennine fells puts the train into perspective, working a special on the Settle & Carlisle line. The models would be set off to the best advantage with the addition of a back scene.

of these sceptical modellers, and show that a reasonable back scene can be achieved, even by someone with limited artistic skills. For a number of reasons, it is not wise to rely on those pre-printed back scenes. Most of the early ones on the market are crude and far too bright, while others, including the new photographic samples, tend to create a repetitive-looking back scene. Hopefully, this book will inspire you to produce your own individual back scene to suit your own personal requirements. It also aims to help those who are completely new to the hobby, who might be starting a layout for the first time.

My intention is to guide both the novice and the more experienced modeller towards considering the back scene as an integral part when planning a layout. It is always important to consider the layout as a whole. A more haphazard approach will tend to result in disappointment and possibly a total loss of interest in the hobby. Using this book, both beginners and experienced modellers with little faith in their artistic ability should be able to execute a back scene that will give that finishing touch to a layout.

Scenic modelling, which includes the back scene, can also play a vital role in the creation of dioramas that have no connection with model railways. The same artistic elements of the hobby will apply to creating, for example, dioramas to set off military models and war gaming sets. Those interested in the doll's house and the miniature world will also benefit from advice about how to provide a realistic back scene.

It is always worth thinking about how to present models that may have taken many hours to produce. Like actors on a stage, models need to be provided with a set. A stage is dressed in such a way as to represent a location in which the actors can perform. The same principles apply to model layouts or dioramas: trains will enter and leave from the wings and 'perform' on the stage set, and the back drop will always be an important factor, giving the audience visual information about the location.

This book will examine both rural and urban landscapes, and will take a look at various skies. It will show how to execute a back scene using paint, but, before any painting is done, there are choices to be made regarding the different materials on which the

Martin Nield's pre-grouping 'Eccleston' layout. With the back scene boards removed at the station end of the layout, the operators are in full view, along with anything in the background. This creates a distraction away from the model, but it is the way a great number of layouts are presented at exhibitions. The layout looks unfinished, but the problem could easily be remedied by installing a back scene.

All layouts will benefit from having a back scene. Martin Nield's 'Eccleston' layout is greatly improved on the right-hand side with the back scene boards reinstated.

scene can be created. The various paint mediums will also be examined before advice is given on how to apply the paint on to the background material in order to achieve the best results. Further chapters will take a look at projects, where paint mediums have been used to execute both rural and urban back scenes. One chapter will cover the use of photography as an alternative medium. With recent advances in technology this has become a more viable option, with its own particular advantages and disadvantages. A few ready-made photographic back scenes have begun to creep on to the market, and these will be assessed too.

A subsequent chapter will examine the important area of transition, where the three-dimensional modelling needs to blend with the two-dimensional back scene. The information will cover both the rural and urban scene, along with the successful treatment of low- and half-relief buildings. It will also consider perspective modelling, and the ways in which this can improve any model, extending from the model on to the back scene. The execution of different scaling within the model will also be covered; this is something that has been overlooked on the majority of model railway layouts. Finally, there will be a detailed look at how colour will recede, and how this should be extended when it comes to modelling.

The final chapter of the book will look at how to light both the back scene and the model. This is very important, especially in terms of the 'temperature' of the light, which must be correct in order to give the best, most authentic results.

In producing this book, I hope to inspire you as a modeller to have a go at producing a back scene. I am sure that your time and effort will not be wasted, and you will be rewarded with a worthwhile addition to your model railway or diorama.

Happy Modelling!

This photograph, taken at the 2015 DEMU exhibition and depicting the 2mm model 'Fencehouses', perfectly illustrates the benefits of a well-executed back scene. The artwork was painted by Mike Raithby and blends superbly with the modelled landscape running up to it.

A locomotive running light engine set, with a backdrop showing how the edge of the urban spread of terraced housing blends into the rural countryside. The location is Haworth on the Keighley & Worth Valley Railway.

CHAPTER ONE

A QUESTION
OF LANDSCAPE

RURAL LANDSCAPES

The first part of this chapter will take a look at a selection of rural landscapes. It will give the modeller reference material for producing a back scene, but the choice of whether to model a prototype or to come up with a fictitious location will be up to the individual modeller. Anyone wishing to model a prototype will need to replicate a landscape on the back scene to represent that particular location. If you choose to model a fictitious location, however, then the back scene need only create a feel for that location. It is recommended that you use plenty of extra reference material alongside the selection presented here, in order to create a realistic representation. Just because you are creating a fictitious layout or diorama, you should not be tempted to rely on guess work.

The best way to obtain reference material when planning a back scene for a rural setting is go out in the field and photograph the landscape of your chosen location. Try and find a point where there are no obstructions in the way, giving you a good open vista or wide panorama of the landscape required. You might need to mount your camera on a tripod, or support the camera on a wall or something similar. This way you can take a series of photographs that will give you a complete panoramic view when fitted together. Modern cameras and smartphones usually offer a special setting that will allow you to make one panoramic shot, by holding the camera or phone steady.

Any photographs you take in this context will be used only for reference, to help you create your back scene using paint. Photography may be used as the medium to create a complete back scene; this will be covered in a later chapter.

It is a good idea always to carry a camera with you, to get into the habit of recording the world outside the model room. You never know when you might come across a scene that suits your purpose perfectly.

Other forms of reference material include books, postcards and brochures. Brochures are obtainable for free from any tourist information office and may even be used to cut and paste a back scene, although you should not be tempted to rely totally on this approach. Landscape photography books from your local library are also worth looking through.

An archive photograph showing Peel station on the Isle of Man, full of useful visual reference for the modeller presenting a quayside location. The buildings on top of the hillside would make an ideal back scene, blending perfectly with the industrial buildings and structures, including the gasometer at the rear of the station yard. Modelled well, these would provide an effective transition between the three-dimensional model and the two-dimensional back scene.
PHIL WATERFIELD

ABOVE: The simple back scene produced for the 'Ashover Butts' diorama. It was painted on to hardboard and is only 10in (25cm) deep. The most challenging section was where the road at the far left runs off the model in three dimensions and continues on to the upright back scene in two dimensions.

LEFT: A selection of printed colour tourist guides and other material collected as reference for a back scene project. The Dartmoor material helped in the creation of the back scene for the West Country layout 'Tawcombe'.

OPPOSITE PAGE:

TOP: Landscape photography books are ideal to use as reference. This page shows part of the old track bed traversing through Chee Dale in Derbyshire. The landscape, with its towering limestone cliffs, was ideal reference to use for the 'Peak Dale' layout.

BOTTOM: The book also provided some interesting skyscapes to use as reference material for back scenes.

obstacle is where the dale narrows and the river flows between steep limestone cliffs. A series of stepping-stones which pass under a bulging rock wall is the only way through the gorge and, if the river is in spate, this section can be avoided along the disused railway track.

Stepping stones allow progress through the narrows of Chee Dale.

eventually the river passes through another rocky gorge which is ... passed over a couple of rustic bridges, before arriving at some more stepping stones below a damp cliff. Just beyond here, by a bend in the ... place you can gaze across to the imposing cliff of Chee Tor, a spectacular place that has drawn climbers, photographers and walkers for ... years.

Chee Dale. The old railway track ...

Edge. Win Hill in the distance backed by Kinder

OPPOSITE PAGE:

TOP: Reference for a seasonal back scene. It might be a refreshing change to set the model railway or diorama in the winter months, with a good smattering of snow.

BOTTOM: A book of pre-war photographs depicting the rural English countryside – ideal reference for anyone modelling this period. It shows corn stooks in the fields and majestic British elm trees on the skyline, both features that have now disappeared from the landscape. The only problem is that photographic reference from this period will usually be in black and white.

THIS PAGE:

Printed tourist guides and brochures can also provide vital reference material for an urban landscape. Photographs of bottle ovens, for example, would be ideal to use in the re-creation of a pottery town such as Stoke-on-Trent.

URBAN LANDSCAPES

Sometimes you may want to create a model railway or diorama set in an urban environment, either a period setting or a more modern environment. The setting might be a town, city centre or the suburbs, consisting of the backs of terraced houses or flats. It may include an industrial setting with factories, warehouses, scrapyards, or modern retail parks perhaps.

Whatever you choose, creating a back scene to suit will again involve gathering reference material together. It might be less easy to obtain reference material from colour brochures or postcards, but books, particularly photo essay books, can offer useful images. Photographs

that depict the period architecture of buildings will provide a good visual impression of the urban environment. This type of reference will apply to anyone who is modelling scenes from the recent past. The urban landscape changed dramatically during the post-war period and, even if a building exists today, it is likely that major alterations will have been made to it. On domestic housing, for example, window frames will often have been replaced with modern UPVC frames.

Industrial buildings and structures have also changed; indeed, many have disappeared completely. This is particularly apparent in the mill towns of the north of England, with the loss of the mill buildings and their tall chimneys. The paintings of L.S. Lowry are a poignant evocation of how the Lancashire urban landscape once appeared. Many other industrial structures that were once common to the urban landscape, such as gas holders, cooling towers and, from the Potteries, bottle ovens, have also gone over the years. The industrial activity of these areas would of course have caused huge amounts of pollution to enter the atmosphere, and the effects of the smoke and steam will need to be represented on the back scene. Methods for creating a polluted sky and urban landscape will be covered in a later chapter.

A modern layout might include tower blocks of flats or office blocks if the model is located in a city, but it will also need to represent the older buildings that still exist in the cityscapes of today. Municipal and ecclesiastical buildings such as town halls, churches, cathedrals, chapels, libraries, museums and art galleries will all display distinctive architectural features. Clock towers, domes, spires, pinnacles and cupolas may dominate the skyline, and you might also consider adding a mosque with its beautiful Islamic decoration.

A photograph of the Midland Railway terraces in Derby – the perfect reference for terraced housing, which is always good visual material to add to any urban back scene. The photograph could also be used directly as a cutout to include as part of a photo montage back scene.

A photograph showing the Brunswick public house at the end of the terrace. This again could be cut out and used as part of an urban montage.

SEMI-RURAL AND INDUSTRIAL LANDSCAPES

There will always be an area on the edge of the town where the urban spread of the suburbs eventually gives way to the rural countryside. Representing this is another option available, especially to the railway modeller, along with local industry. The quarrying and mining of minerals such as coal, iron ore, limestone, china clay and slate would be a common sight in certain areas, and these activities would result in the need for vast tips of the waste materials, which were very prominent in certain landscapes. The iron and steel industries would also create a fair amount of waste in the form of slag. The railways would have served this industry of course, so it is always worth including features such as these on a semi-rural or industrial back scene.

From the 1920s onwards in Britain, housing estates began to encroach on the rural landscape. Council housing was built to accommodate miners, quarry workers and steel workers together with their families. This type of housing often incorporated allotment gardens too. In mining communities, pigeon fancying was a popular pastime, along with the allotments, therefore these areas also featured the distinctive decorated pigeon coops.

In recent times, more estates and housing developments have been built on the edge of towns and cities to cater to an ever-growing population. This type of housing is definitely worth including on this choice of back scene.

Sporting and other recreational facilities tend to be found on the edge of the towns. Football grounds for instance were positioned in the industrial suburbs of the towns and cities, with some even backing on to the railways – Bolton Wanderers' original ground Burnden Park, and Blackpool's Bloomfield Road immediately come to mind. A sports ground with its stands and floodlight pylons makes an interesting feature on an urban back scene. It does not have to be football; rugby or cricket grounds might be an alternative. Recreational parks with pitches could also be included, or modern sporting stadiums might appeal to those modelling the railways of today. Whatever your choice or period for your model a sports stadium of some kind would certainly become a talking point.

COASTAL BACK SCENES

The location of your model railway may require a coastal or river estuary as a back drop, while in a rural setting perhaps a lake or sea loch would be a refreshing option. This choice does not have to be totally rural; it can be urban as well. Your railway could have connections with commercial docks for instance, or it might connect to a ferry terminal. For example, you

A scene close to the centre of Mansfield, showing the backs of business premises in the area dominated by the railway viaduct. This would provide the perfect reference for an urban back scene, with the opportunity to represent a railway in two dimensions, if the viaduct is included.

Modern industrial features are always worth considering on a layout set in more recent years. The shiny aluminium malt silos dominate the urban skyline of a brewery town such as Burton-on-Trent.

might model Kingswear, with the estuary of the River Dart forming the back drop, while Ryde on the Isle of Wight or Lymington on the mainland would both include the Solent as the back scene. Indeed, there are quite a few prototype examples where main lines and branch lines hug the edge of the sea or a river estuary. The stretch between Star Cross and Teignmouth would be the obvious choice for a main line, with both the Exe estuary and the open sea of Torbay

supplying the back drop. The majority of layouts depicting this coastal stretch are viewed from the sea, looking inland, but there is no reason why this could be turned around, to look from the land and out to the sea or the Exe estuary. One of the finest layouts of the last thirty years, 'Bramblewick', created by the late Tom Harland, uses this concept to perfection. The layout is based on the branch line built by the North Eastern Railway between Scarborough and Saltburn,

A reference image depicting industry from the past, taken at the Black Country Living Museum, showing the iron forges that were once a common feature of this part of the world.

An archive photograph of Peel on the Isle of Man. It is full of reference for the modeller, showing how the industry is contained close to the railway, while the background is dominated by the rugged hillsides. It is a good example of the way in which an urban and industrial scene can soon give way to a rural environment. PHIL WATERFIELD

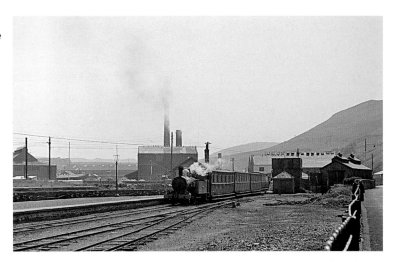

and its creator has successfully used the coastal section around Robin Hood's Bay, with the cliffs and the North Sea providing the perfect back scene.

SEASONS OF THE YEAR

When constructing a model railway or building a diorama for a collection of models, it is always worth considering the season of the year in which it is set. This choice will of course have an impact on the back scene. The instinct almost always seems to be to set a layout in the summer months, with full foliage on the trees and the greenest grass growing on the embankments. Perhaps when it comes to building a model railway, a modeller is subconsciously harking back to the halcyon days of childhood summers, when the sun seemed to always shine.

It would make a refreshing change to create a model railway or diorama set in the winter months of the year. A snow scene would be the obvious choice, but, for most of the winter, frost would be seen much more often than snow. It is also worth considering the transition months of November and March, when autumn recedes into winter or winter awakens into spring.

Reference material for the rich golden colours of autumn. There is always the option to set a model railway or diorama in a different season of the year, and this will of course carry on to the back scene.

Another reference photograph showing the golden and russet colours seen on the trees and foliage during the autumn.

When it comes to producing a wintry back scene the same techniques will be used, whether you choose to paint or use photography. With the lack of foliage on the deciduous trees, there will be less colour in the scene, so photography may be the preferred approach. Of course, this will need to be carried out at the appropriate time of year. If you decide to show frost or snow on your painted back scene, this can be done by applying white highlights to the branches of the trees, and to hedges and fields. The highlights will also need to be picked out on any buildings or other structures, paying special attention to any roofs.

For an autumn setting, the back scene will be very important, especially when depicting a rural scene. It

Reference photograph showing the deep greens of the foliage of summer months.

Another panorama showing the colours of summer. Also worth noting are the large blue skyscapes found at this time of the year. This is all good reference material for the modeller who wishes to depict a summer setting for a model railway or diorama.

Setting a model in winter will make an interesting change, and this frosty rural scene shows how a landscape is 'diffused' by cold air conditions. This may be replicated on the back scene by using a light coating of white spray paint, or some kind of diffusion software in the case of a digital photographic back scene.

should feature a broad spectrum of russet and gold colours in the foliage, which will need to be executed using subtle shades.

Spring and summer scenes will demand a variety of greens, particularly in a rural setting, with the greens of spring being fresher and brighter than those of the later months. Farmland will change over the summer months, too, with crops such as wheat, barley and oats turning from green in the spring to golden in late summer, before harvesting. If your model has

LEFT: *A rural winter scene can be replicated effectively on the model if care is taken when working on the transition between the three-dimensional modelling and the painted two-dimensional backcloth.*

BELOW: *Another summer landscape showing the grouping of trees in full foliage and a blue summer sky, complete with light fluffy clouds.*

A reference image of a small wood with the trees in full foliage.

a modern rural setting, it is worth considering the inclusion of bright yellow oilseed rape flowers, which are increasingly evident in the countryside during late April and May.

Whatever period, season, or theme you wish to model, with a little research and determination you can create a reasonable back scene to complement it.

*ABOVE: **A summer scene, with the whole rural panorama depicted, including fields scattered with trees and the skyline receding away into the distance.***

*BELOW: **A painted backcloth that was commissioned for Julian Birley's 7mm 'Evercreech New' layout, displaying the rolling hills, woodland and the odd farmstead of this part of rural Somerset. The colour was purposely dulled so as not to overpower the model in front of it. The backcloth was painted as a whole, on a 40-ft (12-m) long roll of canvas and then glued to plywood backing boards.***

OPPOSITE PAGE:

TOP: *A back scene painted with oil paint, this time on to sheets of canvas board.*

BOTTOM: *A rural Devonshire backcloth brought together with the three-dimensional model of a Devon farmyard. The image shows how the models can be set off by a well-executed back scene.* ANDY YORK (BRM)

THIS PAGE:

BELOW: *The back scene painted for the Mickleover Model Railway Group for their OO layout 'Duffield'. The end of the layout was tackled using the back scene together with the over bridge to create a visual break between the layout and the fiddle yard at the back.*

BOTTOM: *Part of the full length at the rear of the back scene for 'Duffield'. The semi-rural scene was painted using both acrylic and oils straight on to primed sheets of plywood. The sky was all put in using Halfords acrylic car sprays.*

LEFT: *A back scene seen at Mansfield model railway exhibition, showing how curved boards can look more convincing when used at the ends of the layout.*

BELOW: *The curved boards from a different viewpoint. Note how an aperture has been cut through the boards to allow the railway to disappear off scene.*

OPPOSITE PAGE:

TOP: *The rear of this end of the layout, showing how the back scene has been fitted up to the base boards using a framework to support it.*

BOTTOM: *A back scene painted on curved boards at the end of the layout, by Andy Peters of the Gresley Model Railway Group. Acrylic spray cans were used for the sky, and the landscape was executed by brushing acrylic paint on to the smooth side of white hardboard.* ANDY PETERS

The classic Settle & Carlisle landscape, close to Ais Gill. A back scene for a layout depicting this railway would need sufficient depth to do the landscape justice. Note how the colour of the fells in the distance recedes almost to monotone.

A back scene painted for a customer who required a rural scene of the West Country to set off his Great Western layout. This was painted mostly in oils on an 18-in (45-cm) deep canvas roll, with the sky being executed in the usual way with acrylic spray paints.

This rural back scene relies on sky alone, letting the depth of the modelled landscape create the illusion of the skyline.

Reference for a coastal back scene: Maldon in Essex, standing on the Blackwater estuary.

Another reference photograph for a coastal scene, with the Cadair Idris mountain range forming an impressive backdrop. The railway is included in the image, crossing the Afon Mawddach estuary on the famous Barmouth timber trestle viaduct.

Another estuary view: the Stour estuary near to Mallingtree in north Essex.

CHAPTER TWO

CHOOSING MATERIALS

There are a number of options when considering the materials available for creating a back scene and for any framework required to support it.

BASE MATERIALS

HARDBOARD

Any of the sheets of hardboard supplied by the large DIY superstores and other timber merchants can be used for back scenes, but it is advisable to use the rough, patterned side for painting on rather than the smooth side. It will need to be primed first with a few coats of white priming paint. This will give a surface not unlike canvas, which will be excellent for taking most paint mediums. Hardboard will take emulsion, acrylics and all oil-based paints, including artist's oil paint.

The smooth side of the hardboard can be used if the intention is to cover it with photographic printer paper or canvas roll. Some modellers prefer to paint the back scene directly on to the white, smooth side of hardboard sheet, but the surface is rather too smooth to take the paint. One benefit of using the rough side is that it breaks the edge of the painted image, giving a slightly diffused result, which always looks better on a back scene.

The sheets can be fitted up direct to an inside wall without any framed support. However, they will need to be supported on a frame if they are going to be used free-standing against a layout base board. A substantial

A few of the drawing tools that will be needed when preparing a back scene.

ABOVE: *A selection of boards, all ideal for painting a back scene artwork. The rough side of hardboard can be used together with the smooth side; also included is white-primed plywood and MDF.*

LEFT: *To prime the boards, simply use white emulsion paint.*

frame can be made from 2 x 1in pine to support standard sheets of hardboard.

PLYWOOD

Plywood sheet can be used, as long as it is of good quality, with a close grain to the face. The board will definitely need to be prepared with a few layers of undercoat primer. It is usually recommended to use white, although a pale blue or light grey may also be appropriate.

Plywood can be used unsupported by a frame, especially if it has a thickness of six-ply or more. Thinner ply would benefit from a supporting frame, however, which can be made from 2 x 1in pine, as with hardboard.

As long as a good surface has been prepared on the face of the plywood, the painted back scene can be added direct. However, always avoid using rough-quality plywood if you intend to paint your back scene straight on to it. It is very difficult to apply either spray paint or a brush-on paint to a coarse grain.

Plywood is also the perfect backing material for fixing canvas, watercolour paper or photographic printer paper.

CANVAS ROLL AND BOARD

The best material for painting a back scene is pre-primed canvas. The texture of the canvas is ideal for applying both acrylic and oil paint, and canvas roll is readily available nowadays at a reasonable price, due to its extensive use for canvas photographs.

Canvas roll comes in various lengths and bonded widths, so there will certainly be one to suit your requirements. The main advantage of this material, besides the texture, is the convenience of not having any joins to worry about. The only disadvantage is that the finished back scene painted on to the roll will need to be bonded on to prepared backing boards. Either hardwood or plywood can be used, although plywood is possibly the best choice.

The alternative to canvas roll is a canvas board, where the canvas has been pre-bonded on to a high-density cardboard. These boards are available only in the regular sheet sizes used by artists. This means that two or more boards will have to be joined together to make up the full length of the back scene.

Canvas boards are available from most arts and craft suppliers. The best boards for back scenes are

The back scene can easily be painted on to pre-primed canvas, which is available on a roll. The advantage of using this material is that it should fit the full length of a layout without the need for any joins.

those that are pre-trimmed, rather than those that have the canvas wrapped around the edges and bonded on to back of the cardboard backing. The latter can be used, however, if you are prepared to trim the board yourself, losing the wraparound, and inevitably incurring some wastage.

WATERCOLOUR CARD AND PAPER

Canvas may be ideal for the mediums of acrylic and oil paint, but watercolours may also be used successfully to create a back scene. Watercolour is a transparent medium requiring a special paper. This is available in large sheets, or in smaller sheets in pads, from any good art-supply outlet.

One technique for using this medium is known as 'wet on wet'. It can be quite effective, especially when it comes to producing a skyscape for the back scene, but the disadvantage is that the paper will take a while to dry and that it will have to be pre-stretched to

keep it flat. The watercolour paper will need to be taped down to a board before it is soaked with water. The watercolour paint will react with the wet paper, giving a very good representation of clouds. The technique is to add the darker colours using the paint, leaving the white paper without any paint to form the highlights.

The paper will definitely need to be mounted on to backing boards, and again plywood would be the best option. Paste the watercolour paper to the backing board with PVA glue, giving both the back of the paper and the surface of the board a good coating.

BRUSHES AND TOOLS

Painting a back scene requires a good selection of brushes. It is not necessary to choose the most expensive brushes, but neither should you choose the cheapest. There is a wide range of brushes available

The basic brushes required for a back scene project: a 1½-in basic paintbrush, ½-in flat brush, a No. 4 chisel or flat brush and a rigger brush.

More brushes: two filbert brushes, together with a ¼-in angled flat brush and a set of fine brushes, including a fine No. 2 chisel brush.

on the market, most of which are synthetic. Nylon brushes are a good choice for painting a back scene, as they give good cover as well as being hard-wearing.

You will need a few brushes, ranging from a 1-in large brush through to a fine rigger or one-stroke brush. The following represents a good selection of types and sizes:

- 1-in general paintbrush;
- ½-in general paintbrush;
- ½-in filbert paintbrush;
- ½-in and ¼-in angled edge paintbrush;
- No.1 rigger paintbrush;
- ¼-in and ⅛-in chisel or flat brush;
- ¼-in and ½-in angled chisel or flat brush.

PAINT MEDIUMS

A back scene can be created using various paints, although you do not have to restrict yourself to using just one medium. My preferred medium is artist's oil paint, however, for all the preliminary painting I use acrylic, and even emulsion paint from time to time. For skies, I use only acrylic paint, but in spray form rather than brushed on.

EMULSION PAINT

White emulsion paint can be used mixed with acrylic paint to fill in large areas. For example, the white paint can be mixed with purple and blue to use as a base colour when creating a rural scene with fields and hills in the background. This base is then painted over with oil paint.

You can use only emulsion if you wish, purchasing a large can of white and then mixing it with other colours. Most paint manufacturers now sell match pots in a wide range of colours, and these are a good, affordable option. Emulsion paint will also mix with water, so large areas can be easily covered with this type of paint.

ACRYLIC PAINT

Acrylic paint is a good choice for creating a back scene, with the advantage that it can be thinned and washed out from the brushes with water. It can also be used opaque or as a wash, making it adaptable. This paint will take on and cover most materials, from paper through to plywood, hardboard, canvas and canvas board.

Acrylic paint also now comes in aerosol cans as a spray medium, which can be used on the painted back

scene. The acrylic sprays now available on the market are perfect for producing skyscapes. They can also be used on the landscapes, and are especially useful for creating a diffused horizon line.

The basic acrylic paints come in tubes, which can be purchased from any art or craft suppliers, such as Hobbycraft. The acrylic paint is water-based, so it can easily be thinned to produce a wash. There are many types of acrylic paint on the market today, but it is always worth purchasing tubes from a reputable manufacturer such as Winsor & Newton.

The acrylic paint can be mixed on a palette to achieve the shades required. A simple plastic carton lid will be adequate for the job.

LEFT: *The basic acrylic paint colours to use when painting a back scene.*

BELOW: *The skies on most of the back scenes featured here were created using the Halfords range of acrylic car aerosols.*

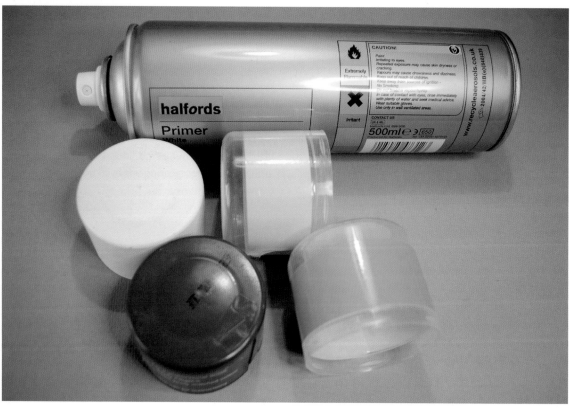

The main oil colours from the tube that are likely to be needed when preparing a back scene.
This versatile medium is ideal for creating this type of artwork.

OIL PAINT

Oil paint is my preferred final medium for producing a back scene. Acrylic paint is used to block in the basic colour first and then oil paint is applied over this base. Because oil paint can be applied over the top of acrylic paint, it is ideal for creating the finished result, for highlighting foliage, fields and any structures or buildings. Details can also be added using this medium – these should be done with a quick stroke or dab of the brush, rather than trying too hard to execute the detail.

When choosing oil paint, always look for a good brand such as Winsor & Newton or Reeves. It is not necessary, however, to use artist-quality oil paints, which are rather expensive. The 'Winton' range produced by Winsor & Newton, for example, is good enough for producing the artwork on a back scene. There are a few oil paints coming on to the UK market now from the Far East. They are much cheaper than the British brands but lack the quality of pigments used, so it is probably best to steer clear of these cheap imports.

WATERCOLOUR PAINT

There are a few different types of watercolour paints available for producing a back scene. They basically come in two different mediums: transparent and opaque. Transparent watercolour paints come either in tubes or in pans, whereas the opaque paints come in tubes or as a powder, usually contained within a tin. The best transparent paints to use are those from the tubes; again, the well-known British brands Winsor & Newton and Reeves are recommended. The pans can also be used, but these give very little cover. If you do decide to use the pans of watercolour paint for a back scene, make sure you go for reputable brands.

A basic watercolour pan set. Watercolours are one option for preparing a back scene but acrylics and oils are preferable, as they create more depth of colour.

Opaque water-based paints are possibly the best choice for the back scene, with designer's gouache especially recommended. These paints are available only in tubes and need to be mixed on a palette before applying.

CREATING A FRAME FOR THE BACK SCENE

For back scenes painted directly on to plywood a frame might not be needed, especially if the boards are over 3mm thick. Plywood of a thickness of 3mm or less, hardboard and canvas board will, however, require some kind of frame to support the boards.

The frame for the 'Tawcombe' layout was constructed from lengths of 40 x 15mm pine. It was made to support panels of canvas board, each of which measured 24 x 18in (60 x 45cm). Units consisting of two boards were made up, with five units being required to fit the whole length of the layout. The frames therefore would need to be made up to 48 x 18in (120 x 45cm), cut to size from the lengths of pine. The right-angled corners were butt-jointed

using PVA to glue the joint. To make the join extra secure, triangular corner pieces – made of a strong cardboard or 3mm plywood – were glued and pinned on to the pine framework. Extra rigidity was given to the frame by the addition of a centre strut; besides extra strength, this strut would also support the join of the two boards.

The sheets of canvas board were also glued and panel-pinned to the frame. The heads of the pins were masked with a little white paint before any artwork was applied to the boards.

Once the first frame unit had been completed, four more were made up in exactly the same way. Units like these may easily be fitted together using either screws or, in the case of 'Tawcombe', bolts and wing nuts were fitted. The advantage of using bolts is that the units can be easily taken apart for maintenance or moving if the need ever arises. This method is therefore ideal for an exhibition layout, allowing the back scene to be assembled and dismantled quickly, and making it easily transportable to and from the exhibition venues.

For an illustration of the construction of this frame, see later.

CHAPTER THREE

CREATING A RURAL BACK SCENE FOR 'TAWCOMBE'

SETTING THE SCENE

My own layout 'Tawcombe' was built to fit within the loft at home around ten years ago. My thinking when planning it was to present a secondary double-tracked main line constructed by the South Devon Railway Company, which became part of the Great Western. The line was built as an alternative route between Exeter and Plymouth to avoid the notorious coast section of the South Devon main line through Dawlish and Teignmouth.

The line was constructed by the London & South Western Railway, skirting the northern edge of Dartmoor, taking advantage of lower land between Okehampton and Tavistock. My layout would focus on the area a few miles to the east of Okehampton, where the River Taw flows off the moor, forming a shallow valley. The layout was to be viewed from the north looking south, giving a skyline that featured the brooding hills of Dartmoor, capped with those distinctive granite tors. In front of this would be the lower foothills, consisting of rich red Devon soil. Small farms and cottages, with their familiar Devon thatches, would adorn the landscape, which would be crisscrossed by leafy lanes and small wooded valleys, all leading back towards the moor.

A photograph taken on a visit to Dartmoor, to be used as reference when creating the distinctive granite tors on the back scene for my 'Tawcombe' layout.

A reference image taken near the Dartmoor's 'capital' Widecombe-in-the-Moor, again showing the famous tors dominating the skyline.

This photograph depicting Hay Tor was used as a major feature of the back scene, extensive reference material was collected before any painting was attempted.

Another skyline photograph featuring the tors, ready to add to the portfolio.

The church in the Dartmoor village of Lustleigh, to be used as reference for a Devonshire village nestled into the landscape along one section of the back scene for 'Tawcombe'.

More reference material for this section of the back scene: vernacular Devonshire thatched cottages.

MAKING A START

In order to achieve the best results, a visit to Devon was vital, combined with an open weekend at the South Devon Railway, to experience some Great Western steam too. Looking over the Ordnance Survey maps of Dartmoor, I planned two walks out over the moor to obtain photographs of the landscapes and features that would fit into my layout's back scene. It was definitely well worth the couple of days I had put aside to do this – there is really nothing better than experiencing the landscape at first hand if you want to create a realistic impression of it for the model.

Using a digital camera, I was able to record all the visual references that I needed to produce the back scene. At the same time, I made a few sketches combined with notes, and collected a few colour brochures from the local tourist information office. All this material was then gathered together in the form of a portfolio. The back scene is no different from any other aspect of modelling, and I treated it in this way. The more reference information you can obtain on site, the better your chance of achieving a good representation.

MATERIALS AND METHODS

To prepare the painted scene, I decided that Daler pre-primed canvas boards would be the best base material for the artwork. (Interestingly, if I were starting the job today, canvas roll would probably be my first choice, as it has the advantage of having no seams or joins.) The next decision was how high the back scene needed to be above the base board level, bearing in mind the space available in the loft where the layout was to be situated. A depth of 16in (40cm) would allow 14in (35cm) for the visual scene and allow an extra 2in (5cm) to fit up to the frame of the base boards.

Ten sheets of the canvas board, each measuring 24 x 18in deep (60 x 45cm), were selected to make up the full length of the visual section of the layout; they would need to be cut down to the depth required. The next job was to construct a substantial framework to hold the boards in place. This was achieved by using lengths of 2 x 1in pine and making them up in a series of five sections, each measuring 48 x 16in (120 x 40cm). The framework was glued directly to the back of the canvas boards using PVA. When the glue was dry, small panel pins were added to secure the boards to the frame. An extra brace was added to the centre of each section, using another length of pine; this would support the canvas boards where they joined up in the centre of each section. For extra strength and to avoid any twisting, small triangles of 3-ply were fitted to the corners of the frames.

The final job was to trim off the 2in (5cm) of surplus board, using a Stanley knife. It is very important not to rush this sort of work, instead making a series of cuts with a knife until a neat cut is achieved.

Once the frame was complete, it could be offered up into the final position, and two holes were marked and then drilled in the sides to accommodate 3in bolts with wing-nut fastenings. This method makes it easy to fit the sections together, and take apart again if the need arises.

With all the panels in position up against the frame of the base boards, the whole assembly needed to be prepared to receive the artwork. I used white wood filler first to fill any joins and go over the heads of the panel pins, and any other slight defects. The boards were then painted using a white primer. The result was a very long canvas ready to receive the artwork.

THE SKYSCAPE

PREPARATION

Once the canvas board had been pre-primed, I could move straight on to the painting. The first stage was to prepare the skyscape. I had taken plenty of photographs to use for reference – not all of them had to be taken on site, of course, and I had also photographed skies with the right kind of cloud effects standing in my back garden at home in Derbyshire. To replicate these effects, I needed a medium that would create the right soft blend. The best and easiest way of achieving this is by using car aerosol sprays, such as the acrylic range produced by Halfords. I usually use five or six colours, applied in a particular order (see below), referring to the photographs as a cross-reference. When using these spray paints it is advisable to wear a face mask and perform the operation in a well-ventilated room; alternatively, you could do the work outside.

I usually take the skyscape to about two-thirds down the canvas or canvas board.

THE COLOURS AND THEIR ORDER OF APPLICATION

(Please note that suppliers occasionally withdraw certain colours from the market, so these may not always be available.)

Vauxhall Nordic Blue was applied first, to create the density under the clouds. (This may also be applied using a mask, to give the clouds a level.)
Peugeot Wedgewood Blue was applied second, to give a lighter shade to the under cloud. (This again can be used with a mask to create a level to the clouds.)
Ford Olympic Blue creates a deeper blue in the sky.
Vauxhall Pastel Blue replicates the lighter parts of sky.
White Primer was applied last to create the (fluffy) density of the cloud.
Ford Ivory Cream is optional, and may be used to create highlights in the cloud where the sun is just catching the edge.

CREATING THE SKYLINE AND HORIZON

The next stage was to create the skyline, which was painted with a brush using artist's oil paints. This medium allows you to achieve the best results, giving the correct density to the colour. The far distance and horizon will always appear as monotone; in the summer months, it can also appear very hazy and the land seems almost to blend into the sky. To replicate this, I mixed up a small amount of Ultramarine Blue and Mauve with a good amount of Titanium White, and brushed it on to the canvas board using a large 1-in brush. Careful attention is needed, to ensure that the skyline is not produced as a hard line. Using the tip of the bristles tends to give a softer, broken line that will look more realistic.

Once the skyline had been determined, the rest could be filled in with the same colour mix, from the skyline to the bottom edge of the canvas board. Any trees situated along the skyline can be added using a smaller filbert artist's brush. A dabbing style with the

The whole length of the back scene for the 'Tawcome' layout, showing how it blends with the model. This also shows how the hills can look distorted when viewed from certain low angles – something to try to avoid when painting a back scene. ANDY YORK (BRM)

tip of the brush quickly gives a good impression of a tree in the far distance.

CREATING THE MID-DISTANCE

To create the middle distance, I used a similar mix of colours, but this time added Paynes Grey and reduced the amount of Titanium White to make it slightly darker. The land was painted using the same brush as the background, working from the near back to the front, and trees were added in the darker colour, again using a filbert brush. As the trees were less than a mile away from the viewer, they needed more detail in their foliage. In order to achieve this, Sap Green and Yellow Ochre were mixed together with Lemon Yellow and Titanium White, and the mix was used to highlight the foliage of the trees on the side that would be catching the light. Hedgerows and other field boundaries were added, and the hedge foliage was highlighted in a similar way.

Buildings in the mid-ground were created using a small chisel brush or one of the angle-tipped brushes

that are now available; if you are not sufficiently confident, they can be drawn with a pencil first. Always draw any buildings in the three-quarter profile, so that they look correct from different viewpoints. Try to be aware of the scale of the building in relation to the trees and other land features nearby. The buildings may be painted in a grey monotone first, and then finished in colours that are appropriate to the masonry and roofing materials used. The walls need to be painted with one in light and one in shade. Any windows or doors at this distance will appear as a small blob.

With the buildings in position, the fields can be highlighted using the same colours as for the foliage of the trees and hedgerows.

THE FOREGROUND

The base colour for the foreground needs to be even darker than in the mid-ground, and it is also necessary to create a depth in the foliage of the trees in this area. I used the same technique as before, taking a larger brush and adding more Paynes Grey to the mix,

The back scene to 'Tawcombe' shown to its best advantage, with the goods yard in the foreground and the station taking the mid-ground. The back scene gives a good impression of depth to the model. ANDY YORK (BRM)

Again, in this view of a local stopping train entering 'Tawcombe', the back scene gives depth to the model. Unfortunately, from this angle the perspective makes the tors in the distance appear too steep – this should have been addressed at an earlier stage of the creation of the layout. ANDY YORK (BRM)

to create the depth required. The trees then need to be highlighted with green or ochre shades to create the foliage; this will always appear lighter and brighter than on the trees in the mid-ground. At this distance some of the branches and trunks may be visible and these can be painted in using a rigger brush (a paint-brush with long bristles). The rigger brush can be used to put in any telegraph poles and fence posts, painting them in the dark shades first and then highlighting on one side only. Fields should be highlighted, as well as hedgerows and bushes, and so on. Any buildings in the foreground should be painted with more detail, but it is important not to be tempted to overdo this.

GENERAL TIPS

- When painting a back scene, be subtle with the colours.
- The scene must not over-power the model in front of it.
- The trick is to create a continuation of the scenic of the model, which is in three dimensions, to the back scene, which is in two dimensions.
- On a well-produced back scene, it should be difficult to see where one runs into the other.

The river end of the layout, showing the up express train passing 'Tawcombe Mill', with the Dartmoor tors looming in the background. ANDY YORK (BRM)

The branch train departing from 'Tawcombe'. The full depth of the layout is seen, from the pig sty in the foreground to the Devonshire hills in the background. The layout is only 20in (50cm) wide at this point, but the landscape modelling and the back scene create the illusion of greater width. ANDY YORK (BRM)

RIGHT: *A local stopping train crosses the river and heads towards Belstone Tunnel. The perceived depth of the layout is again evident, with the landscape blending with the back scene.* ANDY YORK (BRM)

BOTTOM: *Cottages mingle with the woodlands and fields at this end of the back scene.*

ABOVE: *From this elevated view, the true width of the layout can be seen.*

LEFT: *The road bridge that forms the scenic break at the left-hand side of 'Tawcombe'. Note that the road leading on to the bridge is continued on the back scene. It is important to make sure that a painted road looks correct, with no conflicting angles. This one was painted bending away to the left, which, together with the hedgerows, gives a reasonable result.*

OPPOSITE PAGE:

TOP: *The village, complete with the church at the centre, has been replicated in paint on the back scene. The reference was found in photographs of Lustleigh, on the edge of Dartmoor.*

BOTTOM: *The scenery alongside the station blends well with the back scene. Note also the station name made up from flat stones, forming part of the garden.*

Another view, showing the allotment gardens running up to the back scene. The rolling hills and wooded valleys leading to the moor are also depicted.

This elevated view of the tunnel end of the layout shows the joining of the scenic with the back scene. The masking of the join has been achieved by painting in a treeline on the back scene.

CHAPTER FOUR

USING PHOTOGRAPHY TO PRODUCE A BACK SCENE

Photography provides an effective alternative to paint for producing a back scene for a model railway layout or a model diorama. The use of photography for a back scene is not new, but recent advances in technology have made the method more adaptable.

USING A FILM CAMERA

A good back scene can be achieved relatively easily today via a combination of well-composed digital photography and skilful manipulation of images, using graphics software designed to run on a home computer. If the equipment and software are not available, however, a photographic back scene can still be created using older methods. When using a standard film camera to take a series of exposures for a panorama, care must be taken when setting up. It will need to be supported by a sturdy tripod, or a convenient wall, or something similar. When selecting a vista for a back scene, always make sure there are no obvious obstructions that will ruin the view. You may have to find a viewpoint that is higher than the rest of the land around, to give an uninterrupted panorama. If you have a single lens reflex camera with interchangeable lenses, it would be better to select a wide-angle lens. However, if the lens is too wide, this could create distortion.

Another important factor to take into consideration will be the light. When shooting outside you will always achieve better results if the sky is overcast. Bright sunlight gives too much contrast and creates

A high viewpoint above the Dove Valley gives a good panorama to use as a base for a photographic back scene.

This image has been manipulated by stretching and cropping, to give a better landscape panorama that could easily be used for a rural back scene.

long shadows, which can interfere when it comes to the presentation. In bright conditions, the contrast can be reduced and the images slightly diffused by fixing a filter over the lens. If you do not want to buy a soft-focus or diffusing filter, it is simple to make one: take a small piece of acetate or clear glass and smear it with Vaseline, or use thin tracing paper. The home-made filter can then be mounted over the lens or simply held over it when making the series of exposures.

Keeping the camera settings the same for each exposure will give the required consistency. The exposures are made working from one side to the other, with each one overlapping its neighbour, and keeping the camera level at all times. Once you are fairly confident that you have the photographs you require,

you will need to have the film developed and a set of prints made. It is becoming increasingly difficult to obtain this service since the digital age, but there are still a few traditional film processors around. Film remains the favoured medium of some photographers.

Once you have your photographs, you can either order a set of enlarged prints from the film processor, or take the postcard-size prints to a reprographics company to have enlarged colour photocopies made. The prints or photocopies should overlap and, if you have set everything up correctly, the images should marry up perfectly, creating your panorama.

The next stage is to fix the joined-up images – either enlarged photographic prints or photocopies – to a set of backing boards. These can be made from sheets of hardboard, plywood or MDF board and

Another photograph manipulated using the cropping tool, to give a rural panorama.

An eye-level photographic panorama featuring trees in full foliage, produced using the same image-manipulation techniques.

This photographic panorama makes the perfect subject for a rural back scene, with leafy lanes, rolling hills, trees and woodland, and the spire of a local church completing the scene.

would probably benefit from having a frame fixed to the back to make them more rigid. The prints can be glued to the backing boards using heavy-duty double-sided carpet tape or a good-quality photo mount spray. Before fixing, the overlap on one of the prints must be cut off. It is advisable always to mark the overlap with a pencil line first, and check that everything is lining up properly before making a clean cut with a scalpel or a Stanley knife.

This method can produce a reasonable back scene, as long as you take your time and are careful when making the exposures. Unlike digital photography, film photography does not give you the opportunity to view your images before processing the film.

PHOTO MONTAGE AND DÉCOUPAGE

Another way of producing a photographic back scene is either by using photo montage or taking this method a stage further by using découpage.

PHOTO MONTAGE

A montage can be made from cutting out a number of photographs and pasting them together. These can be your own photographic prints or images from magazines or other such printed material. You could also mix cut-out photographs with part-painted back scenes, using a method that was successfully employed by Graham Hedges for his South London-based layout 'Stoney Lane Depot'.

Montages such as this will require careful planning and splicing together. If the colour tones, lighting and angles are not consistent with each other, the back scene will look totally wrong. Unlike digital photography, there is no room for manipulation with this process, so it is important to make the right choice of images from the beginning. Another consideration will be the finish of the photographs or printed material – using matt or semi-matt images will prevent any unsightly reflections.

Once the photographic or printed images have been selected, they need to be carefully cut out using

ABOVE: The starting point for a photo-montage back scene; a selection of photographic prints sorted ready for use.

LEFT: The photograph of the church has been selected to be cut out.

a scalpel, or a hobby knife with a sharp blade fitted, and then pasted on to the background in the right positions. Although you will usually need to assemble a combination of images in order to create the background, you may occasionally be able to use one image. This can be purposely photographed or you might be lucky enough to find a pre-printed image to suit your requirements.

It will always be difficult to find a background image that does not require any extra work. The photographs selected for use as a background will need to be enlarged to the desired size, either directly from the negatives or by colour photocopying. In the case of pre-printed images from magazines or other sources, photocopying will be the only option for enlargements.

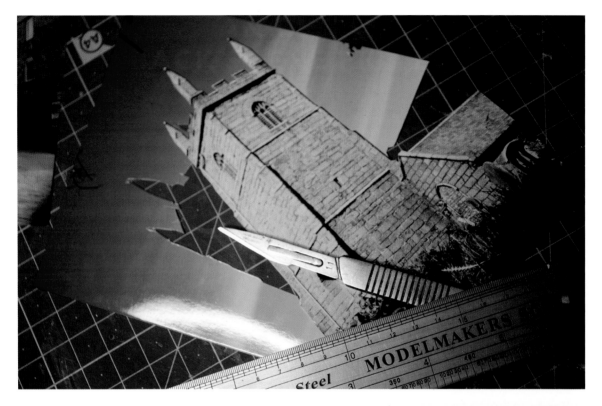

ABOVE: **Using a sharp scalpel and metal ruler, the church tower has been cut away from the background.**

RIGHT: **The church tower has been completely cut out and awaits pasting.**

Trees, buildings and other features will have to be cut out and pasted in position. This is a challenging task, especially when cutting around any foliage and other details. You will also have to be aware of lighting, colour tones and any conflicting angles again.

Splicing together background images to achieve a frieze, stretching for the total length of the layout, requires very careful planning. The aim is to execute the process so that the joins are almost invisible.

When it comes to the skyscape, unless you are able to find it in one image, it might be better to create it from paint, using one shade of light grey or blue. Alternatively, car spray paints or an airbrush may be used to create a realistic sky with reasonable cloud effects.

ABOVE: **The church tower can now be positioned on the back scene.**

ABOVE RIGHT: **Check the cut-out to make sure the edges are clean.**

An enlarged photocopy may be used for an instant photographic back scene.

DÉCOUPAGE

Découpage can be used to lift some of the images away from the background, to give the impression of three dimensions, with some of the cut-out elements of the back scene standing proud. With careful positioning, a reasonable effect can be achieved, although you will need to be aware of potential problems with scaling and the possibility of shadows appearing.

Découpage can also be used alongside low-relief model buildings especially when creating a town or city scene. Cut-outs may be layered in between the modelled low-relief buildings and those painted flat on the back scene.

USING A DIGITAL CAMERA

A digital camera is ideal for back scene photography, offering many benefits over the conventional film camera. It can be used in exactly the same way as a film camera to create a panorama – allowing for overlaps as usual – with the added advantage of being able to preview the composition and view the exposures immediately. It can also be connected direct to a colour printer and then the prints may be used in the same way as any others, being pasted on to boards and spliced together. The photographs can also be downloaded to a computer before printing out, and then adjusted and enhanced using appropriate software. This will give you the opportunity to create one long print.

Some digital cameras and smartphones have a panorama setting, which can be used to create a background image. The devices can be held in the hand, but the best results will always be achieved by mounting it securely on to a tripod.

Graham Hedges used photo montage mixed with painted images to produce parts of his urban South London back scene for 'Stoney Lane Depot'.

ABOVE: *Photo montage used to full advantage with a painted sky. The small amount of landscape works well at the back of the stone sorting screens on Phil Waterfields' Yorkshire Dales layout 'Malham'.* PHIL WATERFIELD

OPPOSITE PAGE, TOP: *The digitally created back scene for Rolleston-on-Dove, the work of Clive Baker.* CLIVE BAKER

LEFT: An image of Dovedale created by selecting the panorama setting on a smartphone. DAVE RICHARDS

ABOVE: Another panorama shot, taken with a smartphone supported on the bonnet of a car. DAVE RICHARDS

A view from the top of the Weaver Hills in Staffordshire. Two images taken with the smartphone on the panorama setting were stitched together using software to make a long frieze making the ideal back scene.
DAVE RICHARDS

An archive black and white photograph featuring one of 'Statons' locomotives crossing the River Dove, showing how a contemporary colour image of a particular scene can be used to produce a period back scene. CLIVE BAKER

A recent photograph of the River Dove scene, taken from the same vantage point as the archive version, to provide a photographic back scene for a model diorama. The remains of the concrete pillars that once supported the viaduct can still be seen in the river. Taking the photograph in the winter, when there were no leaves on the trees, allowed for a clear view of the ruins of Tutbury Castle, which made an interesting focal point.

CLIVE BAKER: USING DIGITAL PHOTOGRAPHY AND GRAPHIC SOFTWARE

The following account describes how fellow modeller and graphic artist Clive Baker has used digital photography and graphic software for his layout projects. The notes are based on the process employed when preparing the back scene for Rolleston-on-Dove, as seen on the front cover of *Modelling Branch Lines* (Crowood, 2015).

SECTION 1: IMAGE CAPTURE

When selecting a suitable location, a distant scene is recommended, as well as a standpoint that is at a similar level to that of the railway. An elevated standpoint showing too much of the roofs, for example, will create the wrong illusion, even if the model railway's track bed is set on an embankment. When preparing the panorama for Rolleston-on-Dove layout, the most suitable location was a view looking across the Trent Valley very close to the original route of the prototype. The foreground details were minimal and the distant scene appeared less prominent.

If the model represents an historic period, avoid any tell-tale modern features such as electricity pylons, tower blocks and satellite dishes.

Unless a particular weather condition is required, choose a day when the lighting is even and constant, with some clouds interspersed with a light blue sky. Although a cloudless sky will demand less image manipulation when individual images are pasted together to form a panorama, this sort of sky will provide more interest. Strong sunlight is more problematic, as it will prevent the images receding, which is necessary in order to give an impression of distance. Strong sunlight will create heavy shadows, which are best avoided, particularly for this application.

Always select a standpoint where the light source (the sun) is behind the camera. If the sun is too far to the right or the left, the exposure will appear darker on one side than the other and this will cause complications when pasting the separate sections together to form the panorama.

Ideally, the camera should be mounted on to a tripod so that the same level and angle of tilt can be maintained as far as possible. Three images will need to be captured to achieve the best panorama effect. Some digital cameras are equipped with a panorama setting, which will assist when matching the images if a tripod is not available.

A camera with a standard focal length lens is desirable for this project, the use of an extreme telephoto or even a wide-angle lens will result in a distorted view.

The light density will always change as the camera pans, so panning too far in one go should be avoided. This can be overcome by strategically positioning low relief structures up against the panorama. In the case of Rolleston, this purpose is served by a number of trees, which act as a mask, but low relief buildings would be another solution.

With the camera settings constant, begin shooting the scene. Start on one side and allow a small overlap when rotating the camera between each shot. At this stage it will be helpful to plan the joins where, say, a church tower or similar feature exists – a join is much less obvious when it is taken along the vertical edge of a man-made structure.

SECTION 2: DIGITAL MANIPULATION

Download the images on to the computer and place in a dedicated folder. The digital files are then opened with photo-editing software – there are various packages available, most of which offer the same functions.

Making Up the Backcloth

Images 1, 2 and 3 (see Stage A), which are to make up the backcloth, will be to the same scale and should be sized in turn to have equal pixels per centimetre – 120 pixels/cm is the ideal size to achieve the best print quality. The vertical dimension of each image should match or be marginally larger than the finished size of the back scene.

Create a new document (see Stage B) with a 'canvas size' equal to, or fractionally larger than, the finished size of the backcloth.

Select the left-hand image (see Stage C) and **copy** and **paste** into the left-hand side of the document.

Stage A

Stage B

Stage C

MAKING UP THE BACKCLOTH

Stage A: select images that will make up a panorama, removing any excess area by using the crop tool and adjust to the size required.

Stage B: FILE 1, Bottom Layer, to match the size of the panorama 120cm wide x 20cm high.

Stage C: paste Image 1 into FILE 1 and position to the left-hand side; excess image area to the top and bottom will disappear.

When pasting an image into the existing document, a second layer will be created for that image and the layer will be on top of the existing layer, which is generally known as the '**background**'.

Select the centre and the right-hand images (see Stages D and E). **Copy** and **paste** into the document roughly in the required positions.

Each of the three images will be on separate layers: centre image **(2)** on a layer above the left-hand **(1)** and the right-hand image **(3)** on a layer above that of the centre image **(2)**.

With the centre layer **(2)** selected, position that image to align with the left-hand image **(1)**, and then similarly align the right-hand image **(3)** (see stage E); note that the image has been **cropped** at the edge of the church tower to simplify alignment.

At this stage, the panorama should look complete, but one of the three images may appear lighter or darker than the others due to inconsistency of the lighting at the photography stage. With the offending layer selected, adjust the **lightness/darkness** until a good match is achieved (see stage F).

MAKING UP THE BACKCLOTH (continued)

Stage D

Stage E

Stage F

Stage G

Stage H

OPPOSITE PAGE:

Stage D: paste Image 2 into the document, having removed the excess area to the left of the church tower and align to Image 1.

Stage E: paste Image 3 into the document, having removed excess area to the left of the gabled building and align to Image 2.

Stage F: with all three images aligned, note that Images 2 and 3 appear slightly darker than Image 1. Select the two layers that carry Images 2 and 3 and lighten until all three images appear evenly matched.

Stage G: with all three images now appearing even in tone, remove the layers (flatten the image). The two joins can be disguised further by using the blur tool. The telegraph wires in the top left, together with the fence in the foreground, can be removed by using the clone tool. On the Rolleston-on-Dove layout, the fence was hidden by a hedge so in this case no digital removal was necessary.

Stage H: to give recession to the scene, lighten the image and slightly reduce the saturation (remove some of the colour). In the case of Rolleston-on-Dove, the image was lightened by 25 per cent and saturated by 5 per cent.

Removing Unwanted Details

To remove unwanted items such as telegraph wires that stretch across the entire image, apply the clone tool, which is found in the tool box. In the case of a horizontal item such as the wire, apply the clone tool to an area just above or below the unwanted area with the **Alt** key depressed, then, with the **Alt** key released, apply to the offending area. The diameter of the tool should be set to a quantity slightly larger than the wire itself to achieve the most effective result.

Larger unwanted details, such as incompatible buildings, can be removed by pasting in an alternative image from another file or some surrounding foliage from the same image. Carefully map around the new shape with the **lasso** tool, then **copy** and **paste** into the required position. This will be on a new layer and can be re-positioned, **re-scaled**, **rotated** or **transposed** before its layer is **merged-down** to a layer beneath.

In the case of 'Rolleston-on-Dove', after the digital procedures had been carried out, the finished digital panoramas for each of the three modules were separated into A3-sized sections. These were then printed on to 100gsm matt-finish copier paper and pasted on to a hardboard backing with wallpaper paste. The panorama behind the Rolleston layout features buildings

Illustration I: this is not the original photograph, but one taken from the same standpoint, indicating a host of modern features, such as cars, street furniture, television aerials and new-build dwellings, that are not applicable to the period of the model.

only in one small area: the view looking through the road bridge. The greater part of the panorama features fields and hedges, with only one church tower and water tower recognizable on the extreme skyline. As the line passes from left to right, from the viewer's point of view, the embankment, the platform wall and the hedge behind the start of the cutting all act as a scenic break, thus lessening the impact between the three-dimensional and the two-dimensional.

The view as seen when peering through the aperture created by the over bridge is quite independent of the main panorama; if it were viewed without the bridge in place, it would not appear compatible with the panorama, but viewers would find it difficult to see both aspects in their normal range of vision at the same time. To produce this aspect, the actual location was photographed during the afternoon, at a time when the sun had moved to a position over the photographer's right shoulder and before residents had returned home with their vehicles (another factor to take into consideration at the planning stage).

When manipulating the image, the sky was first removed by mapping around the roofs and the chimneys of the houses, again with the lasso tool, to select and delete accordingly. It may be easier to **select** and **delete** small areas at a time.

Second, the area defining the roadway was selected and **bucketed** with a colour identical to the existing roadway. This also covered over much of the parked cars that were in the way. To match the existing tone, the **eyedropper** tool can be used with the **Alt key** depressed. To achieve a tarmac texture, apply **noise**, which is usually found in the **filter** menu.

The remainder of the manipulation was achieved by applying the clone tool to fill in areas of the buildings obscured by vehicles.

To obliterate the modern dwellings in the foreground, trees were copied and pasted from another area of the same photograph. **Copying** and **pasting** within the same image is good practice, as the light quality and luminosity will match.

'Little Burton', another layout under construction, also features a photographic panoramic back scene. However, unlike 'Rolleston-on-Dove', it includes some distant and some not-so-distant buildings. The original photograph shown in Illustration L, taken in the 1970s, when most of the townscape was still intact, offered the only colour image available. Note that the subjects are in the distance and photographed over the open space of the wash lands. Illustration M shows the image with the overhanging trees and sky removed; this was achieved by carefully mapping around the building profile with the **lasso** tool to **select** the required part of the image. It was copied and pasted into another document and made to match the size of the panorama. A suitable sky was selected from another image and pasted into a layer behind the layer that carried the image of the buildings (Illustration N).

Illustration J: all motor vehicles, modern house extensions and background have been removed, ready for the image to be pasted into the main panorama.

Illustration K: the view looking through the bridge. The finished panorama displays a 1940s scene, before cars were parked in front of every house and any house extensions were added.

The end product (Illustration N) is the result of manipulation, creating leaves for the trees and reinstating the buildings, which had been partly demolished. Trees in leaf, preferably with dense foliage to make masking with the lasso tool simpler, were copied from other files and pasted into the panorama. Brick walls were rebuilt by copying from other areas in the same image, making sure that the wall was at a compatible angle from the sun's rays so that the tones and shadows appeared correct. Illustration P shows the panorama in place with half-relief structures on either side.

Illustration Q shows a view pertinent to a layout set in the late 1950s. Finding suitable colour photographs relating to that period is difficult; the one used for this cameo view, part of the larger panorama, was taken in midwinter, with the remains of snowfall still evident. The viewpoint of the photograph was ideal, with the vanishing parallels sympathetic to the model. As it

showed an urban area devoid of any trees and other foliage, it was relatively easy to clear the image of snow by employing the **clone** tool. Initially, snow-clear areas were cloned and stamped into those covered with snow; for the roofs, suitable areas of roof with no snow were copied and pasted over those where the snow had remained. If the image had been a complete 'white-out', its use would not have been practical.

The next stage was to add this scene to the main panorama, using the same technique as for Illustrations J, K and L. As the scene was being captured in the winter, a cold, clear pale blue sky was selected. A strong deep blue sky associated with the summer months would have appeared totally incompatible.

The terraced cottages featured in Illustration R survive in the area of the town of the model's location, but over the years have succumbed to modernization in the form of UPVC double glazing.

To minimize distortion, the camera was positioned as far away from the subject as possible, concentrating on the block of two dwellings. Beginning with the right-hand block, the **canvas** was extended towards the left, leaving enough area to accommodate two further blocks. The right-hand block was then copied

TOP: *Illustration L: the original photograph taken in the 1970s, when most of the period buildings still survived.*

ABOVE: *Illustration M: the original photograph with an unsuitable sky and foreground trees removed.*

and pasted, and positioned to the left of the original block. Once it was part of a new **layer** (created when pasted), the left-hand part containing the bricked-up window, with the entry below, was removed by using the **rectangular marquee tool** to select and **delete**. The newly created block was copied and pasted to achieve a three-block terrace, with each standing slightly lower than its neighbour, and then the layers were **merged (flattened)**.

The modern windows were replaced with Victorian sashes by sourcing suitable images and pasting them over the original units. The colours of the individual window frames remained identical, as all of the cottages belonged to the same brewery company, but curtain colours did vary. This was achieved by selecting each pair of curtains in turn, using the **lasso** tool, and then using the **colour balance** adjustment.

Illustration N: part of the finished panorama, with a sky taken from another image. The trees, complete with foliage, have also been pasted in from other images and the whole image has then been made lighter to add recession.

Illustration P: with the panorama in situ on the layout, the half-relief building masks a backcloth joint, and a brick wall at the far edge of the base board disguises the transition between three dimensions and two dimensions.

ABOVE: *Illustration Q: the local scene is viewed here between the buildings, with the roadway disappearing behind the right-hand structure. The lorry and gate pillar hide the join between the actual wall and the wall that is part of the backcloth.*

LEFT: *Illustration R: here the terraced houses represent the buildings that are immediately behind the bridge parapet, and are full-on to the viewer. If the structures were angled to the viewer, being so close to the model in front, the result would be unrealistic.*

SECTION 3: PRINTING

During this process the image format will have remained as a jpg file, except during the stage when two or more layers were present, when the file would have been converted to the unique format of whatever package is being used. For print purposes, the ideal format would be a **pdf** – it is possible to convert to this by using the **Export** function.

To output from such files without creating any physical joints, the recommended method is poster-jet or banner printing on a matt-finish vinyl material. If you are working to a budget, however, the individual images can be printed out and pasted on to a backing board, as already described.

CHAPTER FIVE

AN URBAN BACK SCENE PROJECT

The second back scene project to feature in this book is a commission from the Mickleover Model Railway Group. The group required a back scene to complement its 0-gauge layout 'Warner Street'. The layout is totally fictitious and takes its name from the street that leads to the group's club meeting rooms. The brief was to produce an urban back scene that included the continuation of a road that appears on the layout. The road runs at a 45-degree angle at the fiddle-yard end, raised on a series of over bridges, which form the scenic break. The backing boards for the back scene form a right-angle at this end, as they do at the other end. The road end, however, created a perspective problem, as the artwork on the two-dimensional back scene needed to convey a convincing result for the viewing public. (For more on the subject of perspective modelling, see the later explanation on the benefits of using perspective on a back scene.)

The boards for the back scene were already prepared, on four sheets of plywood for the rear and two deeper panels for each end. All the boards were pre-primed using light blue emulsion paint.

THE COMPOSITION

The club members were happy to leave the composition up to me, as long as it represented an urban landscape. The model mainly depicts the London Midland & Scottish Railway, with running rights for London & North Eastern traffic into the terminus station and goods depot. The period for the model is flexible, from the grouping period through to the green diesel transition era of the early 1960s.

With this in mind, I suggested that an urban industrial back scene set somewhere in Lancashire, on the western edge of the Pennines, would suit the layout. Once this concept had been agreed by the club, I began to look for reference material portraying the location. I found a few books in our local library, with photographs of the grimy mill towns of Lancashire. I also soon realized that the ridge of the Pennines – the natural backbone of England – would be a dominant aspect of the skyline, contrasting perfectly with the industrial features.

SKY AND HORIZON

The photographic reference also gave me some ideas regarding the skyscape, which would need to be tackled first. The industrial activity of the towns, with a host of mill chimneys all belching out their smoke into the atmosphere, together with other pollutants, would suggest a grimy sky. The photographs also confirmed that this was the right solution for this particular back scene.

I decided to create the skyscape in my usual way, by using acrylic spray paint, from the range of aerosol paints produced by Halfords. The range of car body colours usually includes a few shades that are ideal for a skyscape, especially the dark shades found under the cloud formations. (One slight problem, however, is that Halfords have been known to suddenly discontinue a particular colour if it has gone out of fashion, so be aware of that.) The secret to creating any skyscape is to apply the spray paint in the correct order, working from the darker shades through to adding white spray to finish. As long as this sequence is followed, any type of sky and variation within the clouds is possible.

For this urban back scene, I wanted a cloudy sky with some darker storm clouds building over the hills. The sky would also require a certain amount of pollution, which would be added later. The first spray paint to be applied, to create those dark shades seen under storm clouds, was dark grey, choosing either a

Halfords colour or Humbrol Matt Tank Grey. Next, a mid-mauve colour from the Halfords range was applied, to blend with the darker grey, to build up the mid-tones to the clouds. Other clouds were created using a mauve spray, this time creating a slightly lighter shade to the base than those of the storm clouds. The final spray-paint colour to be applied was white, which was used to create a fluffiness at the top of the clouds. Cream spray paint can also be used, blended together when the smoke is added later, to give the

A photograph taken to use as reference for the skyscape, being a basis for the urban back scene project 'Warner Street'.

The first board, with the skyscape painted using Halfords acrylic spray paints. The skyline has been started using a mix of acrylic and grey emulsion paint to create a greyish-mauve colour. This was applied using a 1-in filbert brush, making sure a rough edge was given to the horizon line. For this back scene the horizon line would be the Pennines, running along its full length.

Moving forward, the mid-ground was painted in using the same techniques as on the skyline, with more Paynes Grey added to make it darker. Again, a rough edge was created, with a few trees added. The distant trees were painted simply using a blobbing technique with a nearly worn out ¼-in filbert brush.

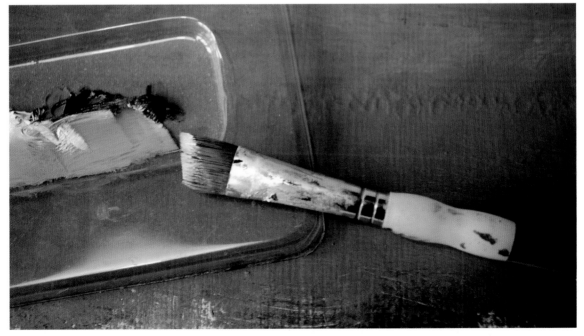

A piece of plastic packaging can be used as a palette.

'sulphurous' effect that is seen in skies over urban industrial areas.

With the clouds and skyscape completed, I turned my attention to the horizon, which in this case was the ridge of the Pennine hills. It is always advisable to look at a few reference photographs before adding any paint. The photographs will reveal that any hills and landscape features in the far distance will appear in monotone. This will be even more apparent in certain weather conditions – for example, a landscape set in hazy light will appear even less defined.

When it comes to creating a back scene, the colours of the horizon will always need to be addressed first. For the Mickleover Model Railway Group layout, I mixed a colour to match something like the photographic reference, which showed a shade of mauve. This would need to be mixed lighter of course if the skyline appeared further away or if the weather conditions dictated. For this particular project, I decided to paint the skyline up to the horizon line first, using acrylic paint mixed with white emulsion paint. (I always use this formula first when a large area needs to be covered, as a water-based paint mix does this more easily.) This was only to be the under-painting and I intended to go over it using oil paint.

BUILDINGS AND STRUCTURES

The composition of this back scene required an urban landscape rather than a rural one, so buildings needed to be added. Those in the distance and mid-ground, like the hills in the far distance, would appear in monotone, although the tone would be a shade darker than that used on the Pennine ridge. This would be the template for painting all the building and structures within that particular area of the back scene.

Once the buildings in the distance and mid-ground were complete, I could move on to painting all the buildings and structures in the foreground. I first drew these out, making sure that all verticals and horizontals were spot on, and that any perspectives were correct. It is important always to be aware of the scale of buildings, especially those in the foreground, which will relate directly with the model in front. If these issues are not addressed, there will certainly be major problems. Any building that is painted wrongly will totally look out of place, so it is vital to take your time when attempting to represent such structures.

If you are not confident at this stage, first draw out the buildings on sheets of tracing or lining paper.

Buildings in the mid-ground were painted in using an angled flat brush, using the same monotone colours for buildings and structures within this area.

ABOVE: **Buildings in the foreground are blocked in with paint. Here, only the first coat has been applied, so it still looks rather wishy-washy.**

RIGHT: **A gable end of one of the terraced rows is painted over using oil paint. Using an angled flat brush allows the straight edges to be achieved without too much effort.**

The drawings can then be cut out carefully and attached to the back scene in position, using loops of masking tape as a temporary fixing. You can then visually check that the scale and perspective are correct. If you are not satisfied with your attempts, the drawings can be adjusted. Once you are happy with them, the drawings can be transferred by tracing the outline on to the back scene.

The next stage will be to fill in the drawn outlines of the buildings with paint. When painting the buildings,

LEFT: *Clear pencil construction lines give a defined line for painting.*

BELOW: *Both the rows of terraced houses running up the hillside and the industrial buildings are painted in paler colours, with not too much detail evident. These buildings are again within the mid-ground zone, with the church being the furthest away.*

use an angle-edged chisel brush, selecting different widths of brush to fill in the structures appearing both in the distance and in the foreground. The angle of this type of brush will be ideal for painting in buildings and makes the painting of gables reasonably easy. The buildings can all be painted in monotone colours first, before refining those in the foreground with subtle colours. The mix of colours will need to replicate the masonry, roof coverings or any wall cladding used.

Once the basic colours have been painted in, features such as windows and doors can be added using smaller brushes. Other details can also be added at this stage, including downpipes and chimney stacks.

Acrylic paints are used to apply the initial coat, then the final finish is created with oil paint.

The finish coat of oils is applied over the top of the acrylic. Oil paint will cover over the acrylic but it is not possible to paint acrylics directly over oils.

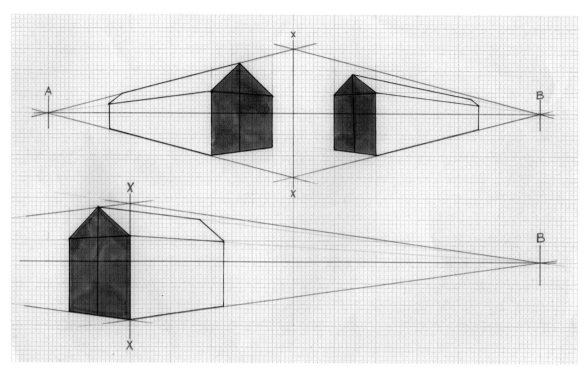

Drawing buildings in perspective, using the two-point vanishing rule. The stages in construction start with the horizon line and then the vanishing point (A–B) is plotted. The vertical centre line (X–X) is drawn in exactly half-way between the two vanishing points before an equal measurement is plotted above and below the horizon line. Perspective lines are then drawn through the vanishing points and up to the vertical centre line. From this, buildings can be constructed using the perspective lines as a guide.

My chosen medium for painting all the buildings and structures was oil paint, which usually gives a reliable replication of the colour tones required. The colours for the buildings included Paynes Grey, Yellow Ochre, Burnt Umber, Naples Yellow, Mars or Light Red, Indian Red, and Mixing or Titanium White. For the buildings in the distance, I used Paynes Grey again, along with Cobalt Blue, Violet and Mixing or Titanium White.

Alongside the houses and smaller buildings, this urban scene also needed a number of bigger structures. The most prominent were the tall mill chimneys, once a common sight in the mill towns of both Lancashire and Yorkshire. For this project, the chimneys were first drawn on to the back scene in pencil. A vertical line was drawn to act as the centre line, then two lines were put in, tapering from the bottom to the top. Before filling with paint it is worth checking to make sure that the chimney stack is perfectly vertical, as a leaning stack will stand out like a sore thumb!

The chimney stacks in the distance were painted in a monotone grey colour. The stacks in the mid-ground and foreground were painted using a pinkish colour mixed from the oil paint, then the tops of the stacks were darkened using a little Paynes Grey, to represent the build-up of soot. Most of the chimneys would have been in use, so it was necessary to replicate their smoke, using a little Raw Umber mixed with Paynes Grey. This was brushed on, leading from the top of the chimney barrel, then blended using a finger to soften any edges to make it more realistic. All the smoke trails will need to be painted in the same direction, otherwise it will look rather silly. The same technique was also used to add smoke to the chimneys of some of the domestic dwellings painted on to the back scene.

Other structures to include on this urban back scene were a gasometer and a water tower. Both were painted using a broad chisel brush and finished with a

ABOVE: **The back scene board nearing completion in my workroom. The terraced houses and the warehouses display a reasonable amount of detail, because they are in the foreground. In contrast, the structures on the far right of the board, including the chimney, are in the mid-ground zone, so less detail is required. The terraced row has been painted using perspective, requiring careful drawing initially to achieve the correct alignment.**

RIGHT: **The paint mix for the wall colour was applied using a ¼-in chisel or flat brush.**

fine brush. Like the other buildings, they were painted first in a monotone grey, then finished with highlights picking out where the light was catching them.

Returning to the foreground, I decided to introduce a large group of malt houses, as these would fit in nicely up to the borders of the railway. These were first drawn out, again making sure that all the horizontals and verticals were observed. Once one section had been drawn out correctly, it was a reasonably simple matter of repeating it several times

until the full length of the building had been completed. Once the drawing was satisfactory, the walls and the steep kiln roofs could all be filled in with paint. The red brick masonry was replicated using a Light Red or Mars Red mixed with Naples Yellow and Titanium White to achieve a pinkish colour. The roofs were filled in using a large angled brush with a mix of Paynes Grey, Naples Yellow and Titanium White. The ventilators topping the kiln roofs were painted using the same colours and brush.

A close-up of the industrial buildings on the board, including the associated structures of the water tower and the tall chimney stack.

The end board fits at a right-angle to the previous board. It features terraced rows of houses again, and the gable end of the pub in the immediate foreground. It was important to draw out the perspective using the vanishing-point rule, with the perspective running in the opposite direction on this board.

A closer view of the back board, showing the relationship between the different perspectives on the industrial buildings and the row of houses. The bottom area has not yet received any paint. This is where the back scene board runs up to the retaining walls modelled on the layout.

When the paint had dried, I was able to turn my attention to adding the details. The first of these were the industrial multi-paned arched-topped windows, which were drawn for one section and then repeated again on the rest. The windows were filled in using Paynes Grey and a few panes were then picked out using a lighter shade of grey. The metal frames were added simply by scratching through the paint, using a scalpel and a small metal rule to make sure the glazing bars were square.

Further detail required on this building included the signs. First, a background panel was drawn out, making sure that its edges ran parallel with the walls and the roof line. Naples Yellow, with a little Titanium White added, gave a flat, cream-coloured background for the lettering. Once the panel was completely dry, the lettering was carefully created, with an outline drawn for each character. If you are not confident about hand-drawing the lettering, type it on a computer using the correct font, point size and spacing. Print it out and then, using a soft-leaded pencil, rub carbon on to the back of the print-out. Cut this into a strip and fix it

into position over the background panel. The outline of the letters can then be reproduced on the pre-painted panel. Once the letter outlines have all been transferred, the letters can be carefully filled in with black paint using a fine one-stroke brush.

If you are nervous about trying your hand at drawing out and painting the signs, there is an alternative solution in the form of pre-printed sheets supplied by such companies as Sankey Scenics. For the large signs adorning warehouses, try using dry-transfer lettering, which was at one time readily available from Letraset in a huge range of font styles and sizes. Since personal computerization, however, the product has become more difficult to obtain.

Signage appeared on a few more buildings, including a couple of public houses, commercial storage buildings and The Railway Hotel. This was executed in the same way as on the malt houses, with the lettering outlined and painted in on a pre-painted panel. Details such as these really add the finishing touch to an urban back scene, so it is worth taking the time to create them.

TOP: *The back board and the end board in their final position on the layout, showing how the perspective works across both. The road, which runs at a 45-degree angle across the corner on the over bridge, presented an extra challenge, as both ends needed to be painted on to the back boards. It was important to make sure the perspective appeared correct from all angles, giving the illusion of a continuance of the modelled road.*

ABOVE: *The back board in its final position, neatly fitted up to the retaining walls.*

Another panel of the back scene for 'Warner Street'. This board, appearing just outside the station, has the sky already applied. All the boards were fitted up on the layout to make sure the skyscape continued from one end to the other.

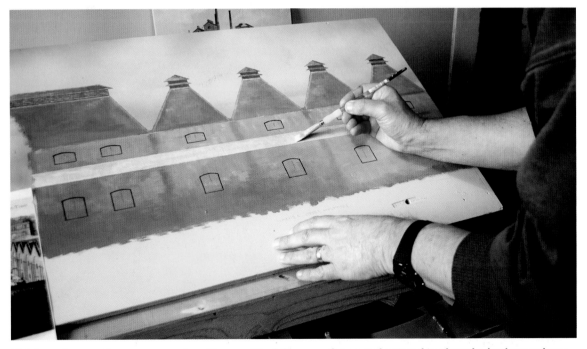

This board was to feature a row of malthouses. The kilns were drawn and painted in, then the background was filled in using an angle-edged chisel or flat brush loaded with cream paint, in preparation for the signwriting. The windows were first drawn in with pencil and then outlined with a fine black felt-tipped pen.

Lettering can be originated on a computer, then printed out to the correct size and traced on to the pre-painted background panel.

Close-up of the drawn-out letters, which are being filled in using an HB pencil. The windows were filled in first with felt-tipped pen and then highlighted with white oil paint over the top half, to replicate the reflection of light on the glazing.

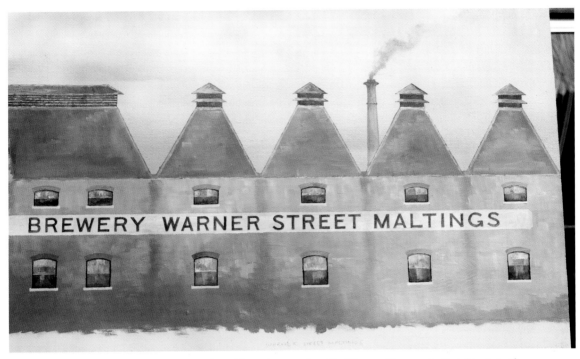

The finished malthouses, with the completed lettering on the side. The malthouses butt right up to the boundary of the railway, so the detail will be more apparent here than on the buildings further away.

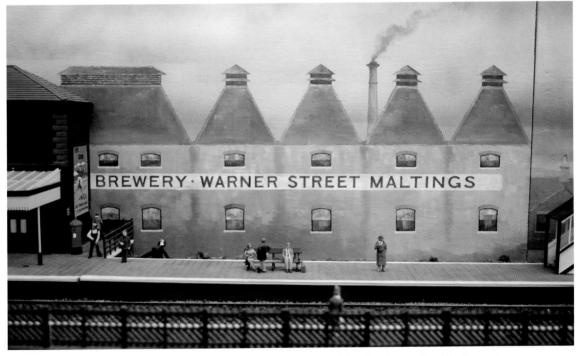

The board fixed into position on the layout, with the malthouses blending instantly with the station area modelled in front.

The boards positioned in the centre of the layout were painted with a variety of industrial buildings running up to the railway boundary. The steam-hauled goods train crossing the arched viaduct was added to the background in order to enhance the urban scene with another railway, this time in two dimensions.

The urban scene is continued on the boards, with factories and the backs of the terraced houses. Steam and smoke are shown being emitted from the many chimneys. The skyline also features a monument standing on the ridge of the Pennines.

A photograph used as reference for the older industrial buildings on this back board. Buildings such as these would have been, and still are, a common feature on the boundaries to urban railways.

The older industrial buildings in the centre of this board, forming part of the rolling mills.

The join between the boards runs along a convenient part of the industrial building.

The far back board, together with the deeper end board, fitted into position. The next stage is to mark up in pencil where the modelled buildings and platforms line up with the boards, and will appear on the back scene.

The sky has been painted in using acrylic spray paints, making sure the cloud scape links with the sky on the back boards, and then the skyline is painted, with the church tower dominating. To the left of the church, a start has been made on the rows of terraced houses climbing up the hillside.

The board in the workroom where all the painting was executed, apart from the spray painting, which was applied in the garage, with plenty of ventilation.

The finished board, with the church and mill in the background and the industrial buildings in the foreground, including the Station Hotel on the far right-hand side. In the immediate foreground, a brick wall would be painted on to the end board to create a link between the street and the station on the model.

The wall was painted to replicate both the brick masonry and the coping stones.

The board with the artwork complete, fitted into position on the layout. The painted wall has created a convincing link between the model and the back scene.

The board immediately behind the station buildings has been positioned ready for marking.

TOP: *The board between the industrial buildings and the malthouses would feature the backs of a row of terraced houses – a common vernacular feature neighbouring the railway.*

ABOVE: *The finished end board, with the artwork extended around the corner. The Station Hotel continues on to the back scene, together with the industrial buildings appearing immediately behind the station buildings. In order to match the perspective correctly around this right-angled corner, the whole building was drawn out in pencil first before any painting.*

The back scene positioned behind the station buildings, forming the continuation from the end board to the back boards.

The whole station end of the layout, showing how the back scene has been painted to give the illusion of continuing around the corner.

The right-hand side of 'Warner Street', complete with the back scene and end board, set up before the Derby exhibition in 2015 at The Round House.

The left-hand side of 'Warner Street', before the public viewing at The Round House exhibition.

CHAPTER SIX

'PEAK DALE' BACK SCENE PROJECT

PLANNING AND RESEARCH

My latest ongoing project is called 'Peak Dale'. The concept from the start was to try to replicate in miniature part of the Derbyshire landscape and to fit a model railway into the setting, deliberately resisting any temptation to be carried away with fitting track before the landscaping was all planned. Unfortunately, it is often obvious when viewing a layout that the modeller has made the common mistake of adding the landscaping as an afterthought. One thing to remember is that the landscape was always there first, presenting the railway navvies with the task of building the tracks through it. Construction was directed at making the railway as level as possible and this would involve major earthworks, with hilly terrain having to be tamed by the building of embankments, cuttings, tunnels and viaducts. The layout plan for 'Peak Dale' would includ all of these features.

Much consideration was given at the planning stage to both the profile and the terrain of the land in a particular part of Derbyshire, along with the vistas I wanted to portray in miniature form. The next important issue to consider was the scale to which the layout and model would be built. My aspiration was to model the trains in scale with the dominating landscape surrounding it, but at the same time to be aware of the practical space in which the layout would have to fit. Most modellers will have a limited space in which to fit their model railway, so smaller

The type of landscape that inspired me to model 'Peak Dale'. This photograph was taken from the Monsal Trail, once the track bed of the Peak Main Line, looking down into 'Water-Cum-Jolly-Dale'. The river has carved its way through the limestone to form a deep gorge and the scene is just waiting to be modelled.

Another reference photograph taken along Monsal Dale, showing the rugged terrain of the Wye Valley. It illustrates how geology has shaped the land and, together with the action of the elements, has worn it away to create today's landscape.

scales often offer the best solution, unless you are happy with a short end-to-end shunting layout. I was fortunate enough to have a garage measuring 17 x 8ft (around 5 x 2.5m) available – it is a reasonable space, but there are a few issues always associated with garages, including dust, spiders, and cold air and leaves blowing in when the main door is open. The concrete floor is mainly responsible for creating the dust, but this can be remedied by painting with heavy-duty garage floor paint.

With the space selected, I had to decide on the scale for the layout. I was tempted to go for 2mm scale, as I could fit so much into the space and this would have allowed me to model the landscaping to great depth. I have, however, been a keen modeller of the larger scales, with 4mm suiting both my aspiration for rolling stock for this layout, and my practical skills, with deteriorating eyesight. In addition, until recently 4mm scale has offered the widest variety of locomotives, rolling stock, track and other railway infrastructure. The out-of-the-box models of locomotives and

rolling stock that have been produced in this scale tend to show superb detail.

Choosing 4mm scale for 'Peak Dale', however, was always going to be limiting in terms of the depth of scenery that would be required, as well as the length of the trains. Careful planning was needed to prevent it looking silly.

The first decision when constructing the base boards was the height at which the track bed would be set. I settled on 4ft (120cm) from the floor level, so that the trains running on the layout could be viewed at eye level, which is of course the way they would be observed in real life. (Oddly, most layouts on show at exhibitions are viewed by the observers looking down on the trains.)

Having the track set at this higher level would also provide me with the opportunity to model both the landscaping rising above the track level and that dropping from the track level. The lowest level on the layout would be the river flowing through the valley, while the highest would be the limestone tor rising

ABOVE: **The distant hillsides diminishing along the skyline.**

BELOW: **A view of the White Peak taken at Blackwell Mill, near to Millers Dale, showing the dramatic landscape of the upper Wye Valley.**

Another photograph, with the limestone outcrops of stratified rock dominating Chee Dale, again taken from the track bed of the former Peak Main Line – excellent reference material for this type of rock strata, which would feature in both the landscape and the back scene for the project.

Common features of the White Peak are the groups of windswept trees topping the gentle slopes of the hills, together with miles of dry-stone walling. These would have to be prominent on any back scene depicting this part of the world.

Another photograph taken for reference of the upper Wye Valley. This area near Millers Dale has been scarred in the past with limestone quarrying.

Intermingled with the dry-stone walls in the area are the many field barns built from the same materials. These simple buildings have now become part of the White Peak landscape and would definitely feature on the back scene.

More reference material for the dry-stone walls and ruined barns.

from one side of the valley. This part of the layout would be fitted into one corner, where the maximum depth for the landscaping could be achieved. The railway would cross this valley on a five-arch viaduct and would be the focal point for viewing the trains, with the track bed sitting around 9in (22cm) above the river below. This end of the layout would be on a constant curve forming part of the radius required.

Before attempting any construction, I planned a few visits to this part of the White Peak area of Derbyshire, not only to take plenty of photographs to refer to during the building process, but also to get a complete feel for the location. One of these visits included a walk along the Monsal Trail, which up until the late 1960s was the main Derby to Manchester rail route through the Peak District. Photographs taken from the track bed would become valuable reference material for both the construction of the layout and for creating a realistic-looking back scene. I also found the book *Through Limestone Hills* by Bill Hudson very useful, and would recommend it as invaluable reference for anyone wishing to model the Peak Line.

MAKING A START ON THE BASE BOARDS

Construction started with an open-topped base board, with the frames made first. A top was cut and fitted on to the framework; this would be for the river bed, at the lowest level of the model. A second frame was then constructed to support the track bed and scenery in the right-hand corner. Both the frames measured 4 x 3ft (120 x 90cm), with the left-hand frame supported 3ft 3in (98cm) off the floor level. The right-hand frame was raised and supported at 3ft 10in (115cm) from the floor level. The track bed on the right was then added on a series of risers to give a track bed level of exactly 4ft (120cm). The left track bed was left open for the time being, as this would be carried on the viaduct.

The layout would have one long side requiring landscaping, and this would be supported on a shallow shelf fixed to the garage wall on a series of brackets. The track bed still remained at the mean level of 4ft (120cm), allowing for a rising hillside to be modelled at the back, with the land falling away at the front. This would give the impression of the railway hugging the contours of the side of the valley. The railway would have to be cut into the hillside for most of its length on this side, creating a limestone cutting. At the far left of the shelf, the railway would enter a tunnel where the hillside extended into the valley, at this point forming a gorge.

CREATING THE BACK SCENE

Before any landscaping could be started it was important to turn my attention to the back scene. This became obvious to me when looking at the two corners of the layout, where it would be almost impossible to fit the back scene afterwards. To create the depth needed for this to look correct, and within scale to the rest of the layout, the backcloth would need to be at least 24in (60cm) deep. If space had permitted, I would have considered fitting a deeper backcloth, but, after checking with a sample section of board in various positions around the layout, I was happy that

the 24in (60cm) depth would be adequate and give me the effect I was looking for.

The next question was what material and what medium to use to execute the back scene. I decided to create my own painted back scene, rather than using a photographic version. This would allow me to create exactly the rural landscape required, and give me full control of perspective at all stages and positions.

For this project, I decided that hardboard sheets from a local timber supplier would be adequate, with the intention of applying the paint to the rough side. The first task was to give the boards a couple of coats of white primer paint, making sure that the paint covered into the grain of the hardboard. Once the white primer paint had completely dried, the boards were offered up into position and fixed to the garage wall using large panel pins. In order to make up the required lengths, some boards would need to be cut to fit, although it is a good idea to keep cutting to a minimum, and making sure that the shorter sections appear in the corners rather than on the sides.

The 'Peak Dale' project under early construction, with the back scene boards in position and fixed to the garage walls. Using open-topped base boards allowed the track bed to be raised, to create different levels for the scenery. The rough side of the hardboard was used and the board on the left-hand side was re-used from the 'Baslow' layout, painted over with white emulsion paint as a base for the new artwork.

Looking down on the track bed running up to where the viaduct will be installed, the back scene boards can be seen only inches away. Once the back scene has been painted and the landscaping completed using the various techniques, this distance should appear greater.

PAINTING THE SKYSCAPE

With the back boards fixed in position, it was time to turn my attention to creating the skyscape. As with most things connected to model-making, the starting point is photographic reference, which I found in a combination of my own portfolio collection and a book of Peak District landscapes.

The medium selected for painting the sky was acrylic spray paint, in the form of the trusted range of car colours and primers found at Halfords. These must be applied in a certain order, working basically from dark to light, the first colour being a mid-shade of mauve or blue. The car-body spray colour Ford Wedgewood Blue matches almost perfectly to the shade found under and at the base of the clouds in the photographs. Another colour worth considering for the under-cloud would be Vauxhall Smoke Blue.

When observing cloud formations, you will notice that the clouds normally sit at a certain level, giving the impression of floating. To replicate this effect, hold a strip of card or something similar a short distance away from the boards, and apply the spray over the top edge of the card, resulting in a diffused edge. One word of warning when attempting this: always keep the card level and parallel with the edge of the boards, otherwise the clouds will all be floating at slightly different angles!

The next colour in the order of application is a pale blue, to represent the blue sky. Again, this was a car-body spray from the Halfords range – either Ford Riviera Blue or Vauxhall Pastel Blue.

At the next painting stage, the tops are added to the clouds, by simply spraying Halfords White Primer. This needs to be applied in short bursts to create a 'fluffy' effect. The last colour to add is a light cream, such as Ford Ivory from the Halfords range – it is an optional choice, but if it is applied correctly it can give the ideal finishing touch. It creates the effect of the sunlight just catching the top edge of the clouds. When attempting this, however, only very short bursts of the spray paint should be used, just touching the top of the cloud formation.

(Note: although the spray paints listed here were all in stock and available from Halfords at the time of writing, certain colours are occasionally withdrawn from the range.)

PAINTING THE HORIZON OR SKYLINE

The horizon or skyline was the next painting stage to tackle. This was first applied from a mix of acrylic paint using Violet, Cobalt Blue and Titanium White to create a light bluish-mauve colour. This was applied using a household 1-in paintbrush with careful control, picking out the skyline, and then with large strokes to fill in afterwards. I again used photographic reference from my portfolio collection and books to replicate the skyline. The filling in will need to extend right down to the base of the back drop, which will

give a background for applying both the mid-ground and foreground.

Before moving on to the mid-ground, I went over the horizon with oil paint, mixing exactly the same shade of colour from the tubes. This was applied using a smaller filbert brush, with any trees appearing on the skyline being picked out by using a simple stippling technique with the same brush.

PAINTING THE MID-GROUND AND FOREGROUND

The mid-ground was blocked in next, making the background colour slightly darker by adding Paynes Grey to the same mix. Trees were again put in with the filbert brush, using the same painting techniques – these would appear larger than those on the skyline, of course.

The hillsides were then highlighted by adding shades of green, made up by mixing Sap Green with a

The opposite side of the layout, showing some of the structures in the early stages. This part depicts the industrial landscape that was scarred first by lead mining and then by limestone quarrying. The processing of lime created some prominent features, including the kilns that were built to be served by the railway.

The early stages of creating the skyscape, skyline and the mid-ground of the old lead-mining area, with its distinctive landscaping and structures. The sky has been painted using acrylic sprays, while the rest of this first stage has been blocked in using acrylic and emulsion.

little Lemon Yellow and Titanium White added for the highlights. A quarter-inch (6mm) flat brush was used for applying the oil paint, adding the highlights last. As always, it is wise to use photographic reference to establish where the shade and highlights should appear.

Any trees or woodland can be added by using a darker shade of the background colour, with more Paynes Grey mixed in with the mauve. This was used to create the bulk of the trees, applying the paint with a filbert brush using a stippling action again. When this stage was dry enough, greens were made up for the foliage using the same mix as the fields. When applying the foliage, the same stippling technique with the filbert brush was used, but only to one side. This will replicate the effect of sunlight on the tree or trees, with the other side remaining in shade, giving a three-dimensional effect. For an autumn scene, more Yellow Ochre could be used in the mix. For winter, the first painting stage can be left untouched, without any foliage colour added.

For this Derbyshire White Peak landscape, outcrops of limestone were added to the mid-ground and the foreground using a quarter-inch (6mm) flat brush. These were simply painted with Paynes Grey first, and then the highlights to the rock were picked out in Titanium White.

The mid-ground of this rural scene also featured the odd building, including the stone-built field barns and the other farm buildings, used by those who were eking out an existence in the barren limestone landscape. All these structures were executed using an angled flat or chisel brush; this type of brush is ideal for this purpose. The gable ends of the buildings were put in first, followed by the side walls and the roof. By painting the buildings in this three-quarter perspective, a three-dimensional effect is achieved.

The trees and undergrowth in the foreground may be painted in the same way as the mid-ground, although more contrast to the colour will be required to give the illusion of these features being closer to the viewer.

TOP: **The boards on the viaduct side have been re-painted to create a scene representing the White Peak. The dry-stone walls and the ruins of the field barns scattered across the landscape have been re-created on the back scene using the photographs taken for reference.**

ABOVE: **The view from the viaduct, looking into the wooded river valley. The open hillsides are visible in the background, criss-crossed by dry-stone walls. It was important to paint the back scene first, before the viaduct was constructed and any landscaping attempted.**

The skyline along this section of the back scene features a group of windswept trees. The reference photographs show how common this feature is on the White Peak skyline.

The rolling hills are intermingled with small woods creating field boundaries – another feature of the landscape taken from the reference material and used on the back scene.

ADDING INDUSTRIAL BUILDINGS AND EARTH WORKINGS

The right-hand corner of the layout was reserved to depict some of the Peak District's industry. The mid-ground would feature the remains of lead-mining activity, while the foreground of the boards would be devoted to the working limestone quarries.

The quarry face was painted in the same way as the limestone outcrops, although scaled up slightly. A larger angle-edged flat brush was used to replicate the

ABOVE: *This photograph of the Magpie Mine, near the village of Sheldon in the heart of the White Peak, was used as reference for the lead mines that would feature on the back scene. The engine house and chimney are not unlike those found in Cornwall.*

BELOW: *Another reference photograph for the lead-mine ruins.*

cut and blasted stone of the quarry face. The technique was to use downward strokes of the brush to achieve something like the rock strata exposed. Before any painting, however, a trip to Wirksworth was arranged to photograph a working quarry. This provided plenty of reference for this section of the backcloth.

The painting began with the locating of the lead-mine workings on the hillside, which had already been loosely blocked in using acrylic paints. To help with painting the structures, I first selected one of the photographs I had taken from a reasonable distance away. This needed to be proportionate to the size at which it would appear on the back scene. The next stage was to use a print-out or photocopy to make a tracing of the structure, or to cut out and draw around. The drawn outline was then filled in with oil

When re-creating the buildings and structures associated with the lead mine, the more reference material collected, the better the chance of a reasonable representation.

paint, creating a silhouette, which was then enhanced by the addition of light and shade, as on all the other buildings. It is important to ensure that the light and shade are consistent with everything else painted on a back scene.

The land around the ruins of the mine buildings was then painted in, using oils, including the waste heaps of discarded stone scattered around the mine workings. The same hillside featured a number of earthworks known locally as rakes, which appeared where the lead was excavated closer to the surface, creating open-cast mine workings. This industry has long since been abandoned, but the spoil heaps have remained and are now a common sight in parts of the White Peak landscape.

This area was finished off with hardy trees and bushes of hawthorn and blackthorn being painted in, scattered over the hillside. This was done using the traditional stippling technique with an old filbert brush, in a dark purplish-grey colour mixed on the

Perfect reference to create this part of the back scene – the photograph shows how the lead mine buildings, structures and workings blend with dry-stone walling and the landscape of White Peak.

palette. (Old worn-out brushes should always be kept, as they can be very useful for painting foliage.) The foliage was added to one side, using the same brush, but this time with a mix of light green.

In front of the stone engine house, the remains of the timber-built head stocks stand forlorn. To replicate these on the back scene, I used a fine No. 1 one-stroke brush over a pencilled-in outline.

The last section of the back scene to be tackled in this corner of the layout was the scenic break to divide the visual part from the cassette fiddle area. This would be painted on to a board positioned at an angle; a curved board would have been a better solution, but space was again an issue. This board needed an aperture to be cut into it for the track and the trains to pass through, not forgetting to allow for enough clearance. Most of the board would consist of sky, although it would require a small amount of landscape, painted using a light mauve colour, with any

edges diffused to make it look less obvious. The sky and the landscape here would need to be a continuation of the board nearest to it. This end board was painted on MDF and was supported straight on to the surface of the base board by two short battens.

Once the end board had been painted, the sorting screens could be positioned in front. A girder bridge carrying a conveyor belt, bringing stone over from the quarry to be sorted and graded in the screens, was positioned running right up to the back scene. The inclusion of the bridge would add to the effect of disguising the trains running from the scenic part of the layout.

The scenic break at the other end of 'Peak Dale' consisted of the railway disappearing into a tunnel. Tunnels and over bridges are the ideal way of creating the scenic break and enhancing the transition between the model and the two-dimensional back scene. (For more on this, see Chapter 7.)

The foundations for the landscape in which the lead mine and associated buildings will be placed. The landscaping will need to blend with the back scene, with no obvious joins.

The whole scene, with the remains of the lead mines found on the hillside to the right. The back scene is still in the early stages of painting, but the ruins of the other mines have already been started on the back scene.

The same view at a slightly later stage, with the highlights and foliage added to all the trees and other vegetation. The ruins of the engine house and headstocks have now been detailed.

ABOVE: **Close-up showing the blending of the landscaping with the back scene.**

BELOW: **The other side of the layout, where the limestone landscape has been depicted, and the woodland and farmsteads are intermingled with the open countryside.**

OPPOSITE PAGE:

TOP: *If space allows, it is preferable to fit a curved back scene, but here there was no option but to fit the back scene into the right-angled corner, and then to mask the corner as much as possible. This was achieved by painting the wooded valley on to both the boards making up the corner, and taking great care in the positioning of the mill buildings.*

BOTTOM: *A view of the cottage, together with the ruins of the lead-mining workings, to show how the model is blended with the back scene to create a cameo.*

ABOVE: *A wider view, to show how the whole scene blends with the back scene.*

RIGHT: *The first stages of painting in the quarry face, using Titanium White oil paint to replicate the freshly blasted limestone.*

OPPOSITE PAGE:

TOP: **The fissures within the rock strata are painted in using Paynes Grey with a finer brush; looking at plenty of reference material will help with achieving a realistic result.**

BOTTOM: **The completed left-hand side of the quarry, with the stone lift fitted. This building has been placed at an angle to the back scene, with the back and roof ridge cut to fit.**

THIS PAGE:

ABOVE: **The next board has been fitted up to the back wall and painted with white emulsion ready to receive the artwork.**

RIGHT: **The join between the back scene boards is filled using a little more emulsion paint.**

The aim of the spray painting is to create the effect of a stormy sky, using Dark Sea Grey from the Humbrol range and Ford Nordic Blue from the Halfords range of acrylic car-body paints. By spraying the Dark Sea Grey first and then going over lightly with Nordic Blue, a reasonable representation can be achieved.

The landscape and the quarry face have been added over the dark blue painted background. This method of painting created the instant depth required for the back scene.

Here the same dark blue colour has been added first with a well-worn filbert paint brush. This technique gives the same depth to any bushes, trees or other foliage.

The skyline has been painted in using a mix of oil paint in a bluish-mauve colour. This has been extended right down to the bottom of the board, creating the base colour to paint the next section of the quarry face. The form of the trees and undergrowth has been painted in a darker shade of the same colour.

THIS PAGE:

ABOVE: *A mix of Sap Green, with a little Lemon Yellow and Titanium White added to lighten it, has been applied to one side of the trees and undergrowth, creating the foliage. The fields and grassland were picked out using the same colour.*

LEFT: *The mix in the tin – a small amount of Yellow Ochre has also has been added.*

OPPOSITE PAGE:

TOP: *The foliage has been completed using a stippling technique with a worn-out ¼-in filbert brush. The grassland has also been finished off, with a few Titanium White highlights.*

BOTTOM: *Close-up of the stippling effect applied to the foliage.*

The rock face of the quarry has been started, using downward brush strokes with a ¾-in angled chisel flat brush.

Close-up showing how using the angled edge of this type of brush can give an instant replication of the limestone rock face.

TOP: **This section of the painted quarry face blends with the left-hand board. A small amount of Yellow Ochre was mixed with the Titanium White to give the rock face a more authentic colour, and to tone down the white slightly.**

ABOVE: **The finished quarry, complete with heaps of stone and the conveyor system to take the quarried rock for sorting and grading.**

Photograph taken at Middle Peak, Wirksworth, to provide reference material for painting the quarry face.

Another reference photograph used to create an authentic-looking back scene.

In this photograph, reference was found at Middleton Moor for the many waste tips that scar the landscape of the White Peak.

The early lead-mine workings at Sheldon – the Derbyshire landscape has been changed by man for many years.

OPPOSITE PAGE:

TOP: *In contrast to the lead-mining areas, the sides of the Derbyshire dales are mainly wooded. Evidence of lead mining is also found in the dales, with caves leading to worked seams of galena.*

BOTTOM: *Panorama of the Wye Valley, with Haddon Hall in the centre. This image shows the changing landscape of the Peak District, with the limestone in the bottom of the valley, extending to the grit-stone edges and the moors visible on the skyline.*

THIS PAGE:

RIGHT: *The River Wye in Monsal Dale – more reference for the limestone crags. This dramatic landscape was viewed by passengers travelling on the Midland's Peak Line, with the railway hugging the opposite side of the dale.*

BELOW: *The limestone crags replicated on the back scene above the tunnel. The reference for this came from visits to Monsal Dale.*

This section of the Peak Dale layout, now finished, is only 14in (35cm) wide at this point. However, with the landscaping blending perfectly with the back scene, an illusion has been created of it being so much wider. The track bed runs along a shelf with the limestone rock cutting setting off the passing goods train.

A Jubilee is seen along the same stretch of track. The back scene puts the train into perspective, giving the desired effect I was looking for with this model.

CHAPTER SEVEN

MAKING THE TRANSITION FROM 3D TO 2D

There are a number of techniques that may be used to ensure that the modelling, which is all executed in three dimensions, merges successfully and blends in with the backcloth, which is in two dimensions only. Both rural and urban scenes will be looked at. Special attention will be given to the ways in which various buildings will fit up to the back scene, examining first half- and low-relief buildings and second perspective and forced perspective modelling.

THE RURAL SCENE

Many modellers attempting to build a model railway will prefer to choose a rural setting for the layout. The term 'rural' can of course apply to many variations

and extremes within the landscape, from the flat open fields of the fens or Somerset Levels to the mountains of the Highlands, Wales and Cumbria. In between these extremes, a good amount of the British countryside features hilly terrain, including the Yorkshire Dales and the Peak District of Derbyshire and North Staffordshire. Other significant areas consist of moorland, with the Pennines, Dartmoor and the North Yorkshire Moors coming instantly to mind.

A layout depicting a rural scene will have landscape modelling right up to the back scene, and it is this area where this book will focus its attention. The landscape modelling may consist of fields, woodland, hillsides or even just a railway cutting. In each case, the blending technique will be very similar, using trees

A limestone rock face known as the 'Scarthin', modelled in 2mm scale for a commissioned showcase diorama model of Cromford Mills.

Closer detail of the rock face, showing how the modelled trees and undergrowth blend into the back scene.

One of the reference images selected for this landscape-modelling challenge.

and vegetation to mask any obvious join. Open fields may prove a little more difficult as the right type of vegetation will not exist. Careful attention to the colour will be required, with lighter shades being used running up to and continuing on the back scene.

This can also apply to hillsides and cuttings, although flock added along the join, to replicate vegetation such as bracken and so on, can create a convincing mask between the landscape modelling and the back scene. Other materials such as natural dried lichens, rubberized horsehair or even cooker-hood filters can be used to replicate brambles or gorse and other rough vegetation found in such locations.

RURAL FEATURES
Trees

The area where the modelling landscape meets the back scene could also have a few trees along the extremity, or it could even be completely tree-lined if there is woodland extending beyond. There are of course many species of tree, including deciduous and coniferous varieties, but the smaller species of the deciduous trees tend to work better in these areas, as they look more in proportion to the model. Perspective will always need to be taken into consideration: even large trees positioned right at the back of the layout will appear smaller than those positioned at the front. This needs to be exaggerated even more to give an illusion of any trees here receding and merging with the back scene.

The natural sea moss ('forest in a box') now available from Green Scene and Gaugemaster is ideal for creating the smaller species of tree. The first stage is to select sections that would make the best trees, then prepare them by removing any of the unwanted seeds that come with this natural material. Before painting I tend to coat the trunks and larger boughs and branches. Bark can be created effectively with a

A corner of 'Peak Dale', where a combination of careful landscape modelling and positioning of buildings has created a convincing blend with the back scene.

ABOVE: *The combination of the hedge and the bridge parapet divides the model from the back scene perfectly on the end board of 'Duffield'.*

LEFT: *The river diminishing into the back scene.*

OPPOSITE PAGE:

TOP: *The modelled trees and hedgerow, showing how the use of foliage blends perfectly with the back scene.*

BOTTOM: *Another example of foliage on a limestone cliff blending with the back scene.*

Low vegetation and rough grassland blending with the back scene. The long grass on top of the cutting was created by using old filter pads.

A wider view of the limestone cliffs, showing how the trees and undergrowth create an undefined join between the modelled landscape and the painted back scene.

If the work is done well, the viewer should not be able to see where the three-dimensional modelling ends and the two-dimensional back scene begins.

mixture of PVA glue and 'No More Cracks' plaster filler brushed on to the natural material, gradually building up the texture required. Other materials can be used, especially for the larger trunks and boughs – for example, PVA glue again, but this time mixed with DAS modelling clay rather than the plaster. The clay can be applied using the fingers first, before sculpting with a lollipop stick or dentist's probe. Alternatively, bark may be created simply by using a glue gun.

Once you are satisfied with the bark effect, whichever method you have chosen, the next stage will involve painting it. Humbrol spray paints are recommended, giving the trees a coat of matt grey or olive green and, in the case of silver birch varieties, matt white. Surprisingly, brown is not the right colour to use – although it is perceived to be the colour of tree bark, it very rarely is, except in the case of a few species of pine and yew.

If the deciduous trees are required to be in full foliage, the next stage will be to add sufficient flock to replicate this. The flock should be denser within the crown of the tree. It is also advisable to choose a colour of flock that is slightly lighter than you might expect, as this will add to the illusion of the trees receding into the distance and blending with the images produced on the back scene.

If the model is to be set in winter, there will be no need to add flock to the branches and twigs of the trees. You might want to add some of the flock to the trunks and lower branches, however, to replicate any ivy or other parasitic species using the tree. Such growth will still be evident during the winter months, when the tree has lost all of its leaves. Observations show how remarkably common it is, so adding it will only make the modelling more realistic.

The sea moss can simply be spray-painted to replicate the frost on the tree, using a combination of Humbrol's Gun Metal and Halfords' white primer paint. Giving the sprig of sea moss a light spray of these two colours will result in a reasonable replication.

Another example of landscape modelling successfully running up to the painted back scene – the wonderful 2mm layout 'Fence Houses'.

Farm buildings painted on the back scene, along with the trees surrounding them. These have been merged with the modelled trees positioned at the back of the layout.

The hedgerow has been modelled right along the join between the back of the layout and the painted back scene.

A fence line being used to create a join.

The hedge this time has been painted on the back scene rather than modelled. Note the careful grouping of the cottages and the trees.

The most impressive section of the 'Fence Houses' layout has to be the model of 'Victoria Viaduct'. The landscape modelling, consisting of mainly trees, extends into the back scene, and it is almost impossible to see where this ends and the artwork begins.

A similar view, complete with a train crossing the viaduct. Note how the setting has put the train into scale with the landscape.

Hedgerows and Bushes

Hedgerows can be used very successfully along the join, to create a mask between the model and the back scene. Various materials can be used to replicate hedgerows, including carpet underlay felt, rubberized horse-hair and scouring pads. All these materials will form the main structure of the hedgerow and will need to be painted, using a matt olive spray paint, before any flock is added. Fine flock can then be applied using spray mount. The finer flocks on the market are best for replicating any of the hedgerow species, such as hawthorn, blackthorn, beech and holly. To model the hedgerows in the winter, do not add flock, unless your hedgerow is an evergreen species such as holly. Frost can be added to hedgerow using the same application as on the trees.

Bushes can be made either by using natural lichens such as reindeer moss, or by using rubberized horse-hair. This can be spray-painted using the same matt colours as before, or the natural colour of the lichen can be utilized without adding any colour at all. Flock can be added in the same way as on the hedgerows, again using the finer flock. Try using a mustard-yellow fine flock to replicate the flowers on gorse bushes, white for hawthorn bushes or pink for wild rose bushes.

THE URBAN SCENE

When considering how the buildings will fit up to the back scene, space will usually be an issue. It might not be possible to fit the whole building into the space available, especially when the structures appear at the rear of the layout. The accepted way to model these buildings is to treat them not as a whole building, but as half a building, or sometimes less. This approach can, however, lead to problems when running up to the back scene. If it is not addressed properly, the building can look completely wrong when modelled in this way.

A gable-roofed building or one with a hipped roof, for instance, will look wrong if the side elevation is modelled in half-relief or less, and the apex of the roof butts up to the back scene. By turning the building through ninety degrees, with the end elevation

The low-relief quarry screens were first made as mock-ups, using recycled cardboard.

The front of the first section of the card mock-ups ready to be fixed up into position.

The first section in temporary position on the 'Peak Dale' layout.

The second section of the card mock-up screens temporarily added in position.

LEFT: *Another mock-up, again made from recycled cardboard. This time, the quarry lift structure has been made up ready to position.*

BELOW: *The mock-up positioned up against the back scene at an angle. The use of a mock-up will help with achieving an accurate join, as any adjustments can be made easily at this stage.*

OPPOSITE PAGE:
TOP: *The finished model of the stone-lift structure, painted and ready to be positioned on the layout. Any mistakes will be made on the mock-up and then corrected before the final model is constructed.*

BOTTOM: *The stone lift in its final position on the 'Peak Dale' model, showing its relation with the back scene immediately behind.*

facing, a better impression will be achieved. If you do choose to model the building with the side elevation facing, try increasing the depth to around two-thirds rather than half. This way, the building's roof will be extended over the apex for a short distance before meeting with the back scene. This will allow for any chimney stacks appearing along the ridge to be modelled in full. By making these adjustments, the model

The large model of the bonded grain warehouse No.4, which features on the 'Calcutta Sidings' layout. The half-relief model works well with the back scene because the hipped roof sections run at right-angles to it.

Just along from the large grain warehouse is this modern metal-clad prefabricated warehouse. The shallow gabled roof works with the back scene board in the same way as its larger and older equivalent.

building will look much better when viewed from the front and from the side.

Sometimes, there is not enough space to model the side elevations of buildings in this way, but there might be other options. Fellow modeller Martin Nield came across this problem and asked me to help sort out a low-relief building he proposed adding to his pre-grouping layout, 'Eccleston'. The building in question was a Methodist chapel that would fill a vacant space, and fit right up to the back scene. The space was very limited in 4mm scale, with only around 2in (50mm) of depth available for a relatively large building. The building would also need to conceal an operating switch mounted right at the back of the base board. The back scene boards had already been cut to provide an aperture, making the switch accessible to the operators at the back of the layout.

Martin had found a prototype from the local area to use for the model, but there were a few issues with the side elevation, as the roof could not be modelled without looking completely wrong. The front of the building included a low parapet, which continued on to the side for a short distance. In the end, using this architectural feature to the best advantage helped to solve the problem. The parapet was constructed at twice the prototype's height for the model, and was extended along with the cornice to the full length of the side of the chapel. By making this change, the parapet provided a mask for the section of roof behind, thus improving the look without losing too much of the character of the original.

Martin's layout features a number of other buildings that fit up to the back scene, some of which were constructed in low relief to fit into tight spaces. A few of these buildings also act like the chapel to conceal operational items, such as switches and, in one case, a mechanical lever frame complete with the locking table. The back boards were cut out to accommodate these, as they are all fitted right at the back of the base boards. However, there is no sign from the front of any of the operational items, due to the careful positioning of low-relief buildings up against the back scene.

The low-relief model of a Methodist chapel that Martin Nield and I built to fit up to the back scene of his pre-grouping Lancashire & Yorkshire Railway layout 'Eccleston'.

Industrial buildings featured on 'Eccleston'. Martin positioned the buildings at different angles, successfully merging them with the backdrop. Some were modelled in half-relief, while the public house and the mill office were modelled in full. Careful positioning can create realistic results, even in a tight space. It is always worth making cardboard mock-ups first, and moving them around to determine their final position.

The pub on 'Eccleston' was modelled in full and positioned at a 30-degree angle, while the stables were positioned parallel to the backdrop and modelled in half-relief. The roof line was continued slightly over the ridge. This always will look more authentic than modelling the ridge fitting up to the backdrop.

Close-up of the same building, showing the roof line.

I have included this photograph to illustrate the problems we are faced with when placing a road and buildings up to the back scene, especially if they are positioned at 90 degrees to it.

OPPOSITE PAGE:

TOP: *The industrial lime-burning kilns, modelled in three dimensions at the back of the layout, have blended perfectly with another building painted on the back scene. Careful attention has been paid to reproducing the two-dimensional painted version, using perspective to achieve an authentic result. The back scene has become an important part of the visual presentation of the Clay Cross Model Railway Society's exhibition layout, 'Hindlow'.*

BOTTOM: *In contrast to 'Hindlow', the industrial buildings here have been modelled right up to the back of the layout. The scene has not been continued on the backcloth, with a plain blue board being used instead.*

THIS PAGE:

TOP: *The model of a pub intended for a quayside diorama. Flat-roofed buildings or those constructed with a high parapet to the front wall can work in extreme low relief. The pub building is less than half an inch in depth and will fit directly to the back scene, making the building look visually correct as well as saving plenty of space.*

RIGHT: *This prototype of the Bottle & Glass Inn at the Black Country Living Museum illustrates the type of building the model was based upon. Note the high parapet on the facia, which hides the pitched roof behind.*

*LEFT: **Stone warehouses can be modelled effectively in low relief. By modelling the warehouse with the gable ends facing, the buildings will blend much better visually with the back scene.***

Another way of blending the three-dimensional urban modelling with the urban back scene is by using some kind of walling. This low-relief section of wall, including arches occupied by small workshops and businesses, would work perfectly.

RIGHT: *Photograph of a terraced row of houses, taken with the camera at right-angles to the buildings. As long as the roof lines are kept parallel, there is no reason why this image could not be carefully cut out and pasted directly on to the back scene. The low wall in front could be modelled in three dimensions and positioned right at the back, to make a convincing transition between the model and the back scene.*

BELOW RIGHT: *Walls and fences may be used effectively to make the transitional break between the three-dimensional model and the two-dimensional back scene. Illustration 1: perspective has been used on the industrial malthouses painted on the backcloth, as well as on the modelled wall and road in front. If everything is positioned correctly, this can give the illusion of the model continuing from the base boards. A: the malthouses drawn out and painted in perspective using a vanishing point. B: the wall is modelled, again using perspective and the same vanishing point. C: the road in front is modelled in the same way. Illustration 2: perspective has not been used here, with the terraced row of houses drawn and painted parallel to the model and the base board. A simple stockade fence, possibly made from old railway sleepers, creates the transitional modelled break. A: the row of terraced houses drawn and painted on the back; photography could also be used. B: the modelled stockade fence provides the transitional break. C: the railway modelled in front also runs parallel with both the fence and the terraced row. Note how the depth of the layout can be condensed and yet still look convincing. Illustration 3: the same terrace of houses has been used running parallel to the base board again, this time with the back gardens also modelled. Perspective has been applied to the garden walls, with the tops sloping slightly downwards towards the houses. Both the perimeter wall of the houses and the stockade fence bordering on to the railway have been modelled parallel. A: the terrace of house has been reproduced slightly smaller the before, as it is to appear further away. B: each dividing wall separating the properties is modelled running at right-angles to the houses. The tops slope downwards to give the feel of perspective and depth. C: the stockade fence is again modelled running parallel with the back lane in between. D: the railway is modelled running in front.*

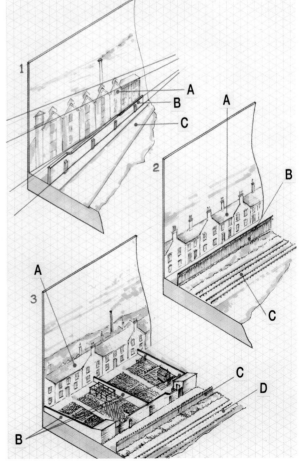

Modern low-relief buildings can work well with the back scene. This office block on the Mickleover Model Railway Group's 'Farkham' layout has been modelled as if under construction, showing its steel fabricated frame. The open construction works well with the backcloth behind, although awkward shadows can be a problem. The lighting arrangement supplied for the layout has, however, reduced this to a minimum.

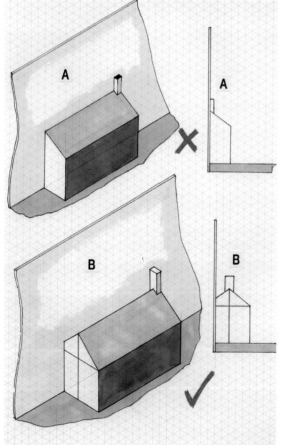

LEFT: The correct way to model a low-relief building with a pitched roof when positioned parallel with the base board. A: the building has been modelled in half with the roof ridge fitting up to the back scene. This will always look wrong from all angles. B: the same building modelled in such a way as to allow two-thirds to fit up to the back scene. The roof line is therefore taken over the ridge to create depth, making the building appear correct. Note also that this has allowed the chimney stack to be modelled in full, creating a much more convincing result.

OPPOSITE PAGE:

TOP: In his modern image layout, 'Stoney Lane Depot', Graham Hedges has successfully used a combination of low-relief buildings together with sections of painted buildings appearing on the back scene. Perspective has been used to create the right effect in this tight corner. Note also how he has curved the road away on the back scene to give the illusion of it continuing off the model. GRAHAM HEDGES

BOTTOM: Another section of 'Stoney Lane Depot', where low-relief modelling is combined with painted images on the back scene. On the church, for example, the tower is modelled in low relief and the rest is painted. This effect is very convincing when viewed from the front, giving the illusion of depth to the city landscape. GRAHAM HEDGES

The use and exaggeration of perspective can give a convincing result on models, but it is seldom used correctly, or even attempted. A: here the building has been positioned parallel with the back scene, but the gable end has been made wider at one end than the other, at the same time still allowing the pitch of the roof to run over the ridge. The end walls are also modelled at an angle rather than straight; this combines with the front wall and roof ridge set at an angle to give the building exaggerated perspective. B: the same building is modelled as

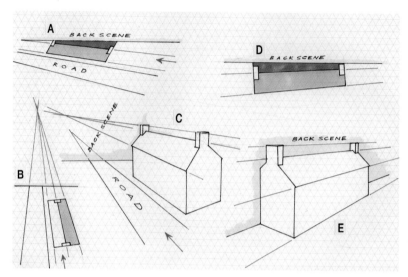

a whole, although this time at right-angles to the back scene. The end walls, side walls and roof ridge are all modelled with perspective running towards a vanishing point somewhere on the back scene. The road in front also continues with perspective taking it to the same vanishing point. C: how the model building will appear in 3D perspective. D: the building running parallel to the back scene, the opposite way on to A. The gable-end angles are also shallower and less exaggerated. E: the building shown in 3D, giving a good idea of how it will look on the layout or diorama.

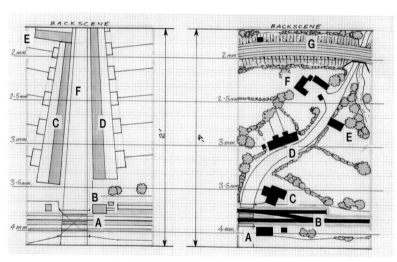

Two plans drawn out: (left) an urban scene based on one of the brewery railway branches in Burton-on-Trent. The railway is in the foreground, with the street and terraced housing receding towards the back scene; and (right) a rural scene, which includes a branch line in the foreground and a main line appearing in the background, positioned just in front of the back scene, with the diminishing landscape in between. The urban scene features A: the brewery branch railway with level crossing, modelled in the 4mm zone; B: the signal box controlling the signals and the level crossing, modelled in the 4mm zone; C: the left-hand row of terraced houses, starting in the 3.5mm zone and diminishing to the 2mm zone; D: the right-hand row of terraced houses also starts within the 3.5 mm zone and diminishes to the 2mm zone; E: the chapel is modelled in the 2mm zone using forced perspective; and F: the street diminishes from the front in the 4mm zone and finishes right up to the back scene in the 2mm zone, using perspective along its length. The rural scene features A: the signal box and the level crossing, modelled in the 4mm zone; B: the railway, positioned at the front of the layout in 4mm scale, using 00 EM or P4 track work; C: the crossing house, mainly within the 4mm zone; D: the row of cottages can be modelled into the 3.5mm zone; E: the barn appears within the 3mm zone; F: the farm will be modelled in 3mm scale; and G: the main-line railway elevated on the embankment will be 2mm scale, using 00.9N-gauge track work.

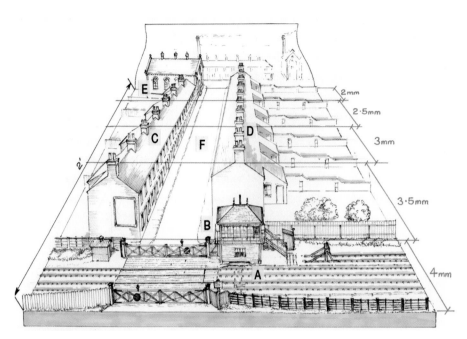

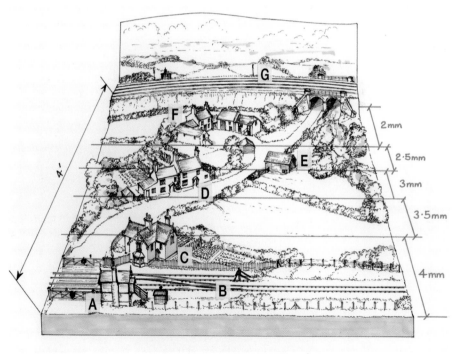

An illustration of the same section, to give an idea how the urban brewery railway layout will appear when modelled. Again, it is divided into the same zones to show how the same features (A–E) will look as they diminish towards the back scene. This is based on the layout measuring 2ft (60cm) in depth with the track work placed at the front of the base boards.

The rural section has a base-board depth of 4ft (120cm), to allow for the two railways to be modelled in different scales. This illustration has again been divided into the same zones, with all the buildings and landscaping features (A–G) to be modelled in the relative scales as they recede towards the back scene. When including two railways in different scales, it is vital to keep constant the distance between them, otherwise the effect of the perspective will not work.

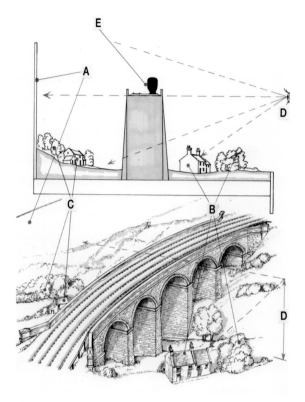

Considering scale and perspective on an elevated railway. Here, the railway has been elevated on a five-arched viaduct crossing a deep river valley. The track and trains are modelled in 4mm scale and will be viewed at eye level (D). Features such as the buildings and trees are below eye level, so they can be modelled smaller in scale, giving the illusion of perspective. The buildings along with the trees in front of the viaduct (B) can be modelled in 3mm scale, while the barn at the rear of the viaduct (C) will be modelled in 2mm scale, because it is further away from the viewing point (D) as well as being lower. The trees in this area will be modelled in the same scale and will blend into the back scene (A). The Victoria Viaduct on the 2mm scale layout 'Fence Houses' is a good example of the use of this effect, although without the buildings.

THE REAR OF THE BACK SCENE

The back scene boards will always be more robust if they are supported on some kind of framework. This applies to both fixed layouts at home and layouts or dioramas that are built to go out to exhibitions. Most exhibition layouts will be operated from the rear, so the rear of the back scene boards will be visible to the operators. The front of the back scene boards will display the artwork of course, but the rear can also be used to accommodate various items for the layout's operation.

To illustrate this use, it is worth looking again at 'Eccleston'. Martin Nield created a framework for the back boards, making them more substantial for transit to exhibitions and for fixing up to the base boards. The framework was also extended with a sturdy housing to accommodate switches and wiring, creating a tidy environment for the operators to work in.

The back of the boards can also be utilized to display information that is relevant to the operators, such as a track diagram locating the points and signals, or a working timetable or train operation sequence cards.

The rear of 'Eccleston' is wider at the station end, so the back scene is not straight from one end to the other. Rather than creating a shallow-angle join, Martin opted for a slight curve in the back scene boards. This construction tends to look much better from the front, with no obvious joins visible to the viewing public. To achieve this slight bend, he used a commercially available MDF that has been pre-cut half-way through with a series of vertical saw cuts. This board is flexible and can be bent to the required curve when fixed into position.

OPPOSITE PAGE:

TOP: In some cases, low-relief building can be used to house operating devices. Here, Martin Nield has used a building to house a manual lever frame. With the back scene boards and the building removed, the frame is revealed; a cut-out in the back scene board gives access to the operator.

BOTTOM: With the back scene boards back in position and the tank house back in its location, the lever frame inside is not visible at all from the front of the layout.

A view of the back of the back scene boards shows how the lever frame has been accommodated. Such a solution is well worth considering when planning the layout, to save as much space as possible.

The reverse side of the back scene boards of 'Eccleston', showing how switches have been accommodated within the framework. The section with grooves cut along the full depth shows where the back scene board curves to become wider at one end of the layout. The use of a gentle curve rather than a shallow angle will always look better, and give the impression of the back scene being continuous.

Another lever frame, positioned on the edge of the base board. This required a larger cut-out in the back scene boards, necessitating a larger building to hide it from view.

The large low-relief mill building that fits over the lever frame. It can easily slot into position, fitting right up to the back scene and totally hiding the frame from view.

PERSPECTIVE ON BUILDINGS AND OTHER FEATURES

Perspective modelling is often overlooked by railway modellers, which is a shame as it can greatly improve the look of a layout as well as solving space problems at the rear of the set-up. This approach can also be taken a step further, with the buildings being modelled with the roof lines and ridge descending from one end to the other – in other words, with perspective being applied to the buildings at the rear, increasing their visual accuracy. The perspective will need to be applied at a gentle angle, otherwise it may not look right. Some buildings will benefit from having steep angles to the end elevations and shallow angles to the sides and roof profile. This is called forced perspective and is worth experimenting with. It is a good idea to make up a simple cardboard mock-up first, then fit this up in position in order to determine whether the angles look too steep or too shallow for the location for which the building is intended.

Perspective can also be used on other features besides the buildings; for example, using perspective on roads, walls and fence lines will show them all to the best advantage. Straight roads, walls and fences will, of course, work well, but the technique may also be adapted to others that are not straight. This will need to be carried on to the back scene, where the perspective modelling in three dimensions meets up with the two-dimensional artwork.

If there is sufficient depth at the rear of the layout or diorama, perspective modelling can be used to give the viewer the illusion of infinite depth. The idea is to model all the features, such as buildings, trees, walls, and so on, in the same scale as the railway. The scale of the modelling will then recede gently, moving towards the back scene. If this is carried out with care, the finished result can look quite convincing. If you are not too sure about how to carry out the technique, especially with the buildings, try building mock-ups first from cardboard. A little extra time and effort here will bring their rewards.

Most modellers tend to model everything in the same scale as the railway, but there is no reason why features at the rear should not be modelled in smaller scales. This technique can also be used in other areas of the layout's landscaping; for example, if a valley is a feature of the layout, the railway may cross this on a viaduct. The scale at track and eye level will obviously need to be the same as that of the railway, but there is no reason why any buildings or other features positioned lower in the bottom of the valley should not be modelled slightly smaller. When planning a model railway layout or diorama, careful consideration of the perspective will allow you to accommodate a surprising number of features in the space available.

CHAPTER EIGHT

LIGHTING AND PRESENTATION

The presentation of the layout or the diorama is an important consideration, particularly in terms of how to light it to the best advantage. Producing a back scene demands a significant amount of time and effort, and it would be a shame to spoil the effect by using poor or incorrect lighting. If you have a large layout, you will have to consider spending the money and time to construct a lighting frame or rig.

Just like the back scene, the lighting and its supports should be planned into the layout from the start and not left as an afterthought. The construction will differ, depending on whether the layout will be a permanent fixture or whether the lighting will need to be housed in a detachable unit, for an exhibition layout.

SUPPORTS FOR LIGHTING

A SIMPLE VALANCE

One reasonable solution for lighting a permanent layout is a simple valance, which could be fixed directly to the celling of the railway room or hung from the rafters in the loft. For each situation, the valance or pelmet will need to include a light frame. In most cases, two strips of pine measuring 1 x 1in (50 x 50mm) will be enough to create this, with the strips fixed one to the top and one to the bottom edge of the 5mm Masonite (hardboard). This material is durable and can be easily curved or even bent around a right-angled corner. The depth of the board may vary, but a depth of at least 8in (200mm) is recommended. This, along with any framework on the inside, will then need to be painted white. The facing side of the valance board can be painted black, dark grey or any other dark colour.

A series of fluorescent tubes can then be mounted either to the celling immediately behind the valance, or fitted direct to the top valance frame. Other types

of lights can always be fitted, although the positioning of the bulbs may be an issue.

A LIGHTING FRAME OR RIG

When it comes to building an exhibition layout, a lighting frame or rig will have to be considered. There are various different designs, but basically it will consist of a series of upright stanchions with a supported cross-bar, resembling something like a gallows. The uprights are usually bolted or connected in some other way to the framework of the base board or the supporting legs. Variations include a cantilevered design replicating the supports used for the grand-stands at football stadiums.

All the designs carry some kind of pelmet or valance across the front, creating a facia to which the lights are fitted, running along on the inside. Again, the inside areas will need to be painted white, to concentrate the light produced back on to the model, while the outside will be painted black or a dark colour. Besides supporting the lighting, the valance will also frame the layout, thus improving its general presentation.

SELECTING THE LIGHTS

When it comes to selecting the actual lights, there are a number of factors to consider, such as lighting temperature and overall lighting intensity, as well as the avoidance of unsightly shadows. These factors will apply of course to exhibition layouts as well as to fixed layouts that never leave home.

Most modellers prefer to use fluorescent tubes to light their model, as these are the best option for the overall lighting effect required. The tubes are now available with a daylight temperature, which gives a more realistic appearance to the model.

The tubes must be set up in series and wired appropriately. If you are not sure of how to do this,

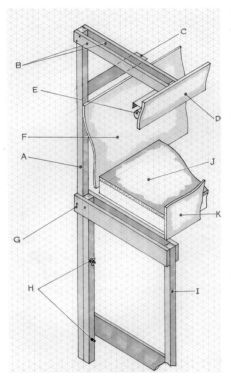

LEFT: *The construction of a conventional timber lighting frame. A: the main upright stanchion, made from 2 x 2in timber; B: the cross-bar sections, made from two lengths of 2 x 0.75in timber; C: for stability a brace is positioned at 45 degrees over the corner, made from the same timber as the cross-bars; D: a facia is made to be fitted to the front of the cross-bars, constructed from plywood cut to a depth of around 8in (400mm); E: the lighting units (in this case, fluorescent tubes) can then be mounted to the inside face of the facia or pelmet; F: the back scene boards are mounted in the space below the angled brace to sit on top of the trestle framework and sit snug up to the stanchion upright, where they can be screwed, bolted or clamped into position; G: the cross-members of the trestle are made extra-long to fit up to the stanchion upright; H: the upright stanchion can then be bolted or clamped to the rear upright leg of the trestle, making a secure connection; I: the front supporting leg of the trestle, made from the same 2 x 2in timber; J: the base board sitting on its under-framework; K: the base-board facia board is cut from plywood. This may need to be shaped on the top edge to follow the landscaping, and the bottom edge will need to overlap the front legs of the trestle. A cloth drape can be attached to the inside of this, to hang down in front.*

There are a number of different ways of constructing a lighting frame or rig. Illustration 1 shows a standard frame: A: the main stanchion of the lighting frame; B: the back scene fitted up to the upright of the lighting frame and sitting either on the base-board top or on the trestle cross-bars; C: the pelmet, valance or facia, with fluorescent tubes fitted. Illustration 2 shows the same construction for the stanchion, but the back-scene board has been curved to extend on to the angle brace. This will allow for the back-scene image to be extended, for example, to include more sky. Pre-grooved bendable MDF board is recommended; canvas roll can then be pasted on to it without too much difficulty. A: the timber stanchion showing the angled brace piece; B: the backing board to accommodate the back scene, using pre-grooved MDF board; C: the facia supporting the lighting, made from plywood or MDF board. Illustration 3 shows a different type of design of lighting-frame stanchion, this type using the cantilever principle, with the cross-bars extended at the rear. Angled braces are anchored to the cross-bar and main upright stanchion, counter-balancing the weight of the facia and the lighting rig fitted. A: the main upright stanchion with extended cross-bars. Angled braces (filled in black) take the weight of the facia and lighting rig. B: this design allows for a much deeper back scene to be fitted, with no angle brace

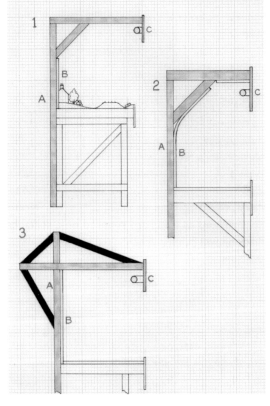

required on the front of the main upright stanchion. This may, however, cause restrictions if the layout is to be operated from the rear; C: the facia board or pelmet complete with the lighting rig using fluorescent tubes.

LEFT: *A simple stanchion made from square steel sections used for market stalls. This has been attached to the trestle using a 'G' clamp.*

BELOW: *Close-up showing how the 'G' clamp is positioned.*

arrange for a professional electrician to carry it out for you. It goes without saying that anything connected with electricity should be wired correctly, with sufficient safety devices added to the circuit when fitted. The same wiring arrangements would apply to positioning of lighting tubes behind the valance when suspended from the ceiling.

Recent years have seen developments in LED lighting, which has become very popular with railway modellers. LED lights are now available as single units of multiple lights or as a string or ribbon of lights. One example of the effective use of ribbons of LEDs may be seen on Ian Mellors' industrial layout, 'Summit Colliery', which is lit by items from Maplins Electronics. The ribbons of lights are supplied on a self-adhesive backing, which makes them easy to fix up under a pelmet or valance. Ribbons can also be easily joined together to make a string of lights to any desired length.

Both the tubes and LEDs can be used for the purpose of lighting a model railway or diorama. The advantage of most LEDs is the bright daylight temperature emitted from them. There are single, round battery-operated units, with clusters of around twelve lights arranged within each unit, available at very affordable prices from all branches of Wilko's and other DIY stores. They represent a very economical way of providing a lighting system, with units easily

replaced if one happens to fail. Many come with a magnetic base, as they are intended for use as emergency inspection lights, ready to fix under the bonnet of the car. This could be used to great advantage if a metal strip was positioned on the inside of the facia or valance.

AVOID SHADOWS

Both types of lighting system will produce shadows cast from items placed close to the back scene. The only way to avoid this completely is to place some kind of diffuser in front of the lights. It is recommended that you use fluorescent tubes complete with a diffusing shade already fixed to the unit. Otherwise, you could try to make a diffusing panel from clear or frosted perspex. (If you use the clear perspex, you will need to add tracing paper or something similar to the outside, to create the diffusion.) Remember that the perspex will become rather hot if the lights are kept on for long periods.

CONSTRUCTING A LIGHTING FRAME FOR 'ECCLESTON'

It might be instructive to describe how Martin Nield designed and constructed the lighting frame for his exhibition layout 'Eccleston'. As the layout was intended to be portable, careful attention to the design was required at all stages during construction. The lighting frame needed to be made as light as possible but robust at the same time. It also needed to be made in such a way that it could be assembled and dismantled both quickly and safely. With exhibition layouts, it is important to think carefully about transportation and possibly storage.

Taking all these issues into consideration, Martin came up with a suitable design for his requirements. Timber was chosen as the main material for the stanchions, using 2 x 2in (50 x 50mm) for the uprights, cut to a length of 5ft (150cm). The cross-members and feet were made from 2 x 1in (50 x 25mm) timber with a facia cut from plywood, which added extra strength and rigidity. The cross-members varied in length, with the widest appearing at the station end of the layout. Each stanchion fits up against the back scene boards,

*TOP LEFT: **One of the end stanchions fitted to the framework of Martin Nield's 'Eccleston' layout.***

*LEFT: **The end stanchion seen from the viewing side, with the fiddle area behind.***

and is connected to the frames using 'G' clamps. Martin favours this method rather than screws or bolts, as the level of exhibition hall floors can differ.

The lighting sections were made from plywood for the facia, with a top frame of pine and another length of plywood fixed to the top, making an 'L'-shaped profile. The end of each section included a wooden dowel peg fixed into the pine frame, which would locate with a hole drilled into the end of the cross-bars of the upright stanchions. This method would make the lighting rig sections easy to assemble and

*RIGHT: **Martin Nield decided to create a frame on the base of the stanchion, giving it a foot to stand on. This was braced by an angled piece of plywood to give extra stability. This is an ideal solution for exhibition layouts, where stanchions have to be set up and dismantled easily, but at the same time need to be safe, without any possibility of collapse.***

*BELOW: **The station end of 'Eccleston', showing this part of the lighting frame stanchion. The inside face of the plywood brace has been painted white.***

ABOVE: **The station end of 'Eccleston', showing the outside of the plywood brace, which has been painted dark brown.**

BELOW LEFT: **The 'Eccleston' layout is lit by fluorescent tubes mounted to the inside of the facia or pelmet. The lighting-frame units are located to the cross-members with a dowel peg.**

BELOW RIGHT: **The dowels and the connecting leads with two-pin plugs supplied. The inside of the frame has been painted white to reflect the light on to the layout.**

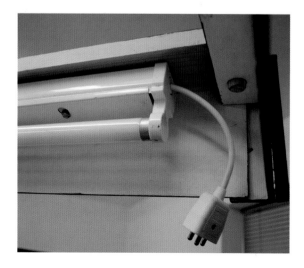
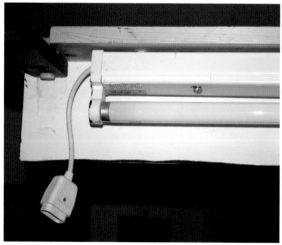

ABOVE: *The cable with the male and female plugs connected.*

LEFT: *Close-up showing the cables connected.*

dismantle when attending exhibitions, without the inconvenience of undoing bolts or screws. The sections could of course be fixed with screws and bolts if the layout was not going to leave home.

Alternative lighting pelmets may utilize UPVC electrical ducting or lengths of white UPVC guttering, supported on stanchions made from tubular metal or timber. Whatever lighting rig you choose to build, make sure that the lights are projected in such a way as to give effective overall lighting to your layout or diorama.

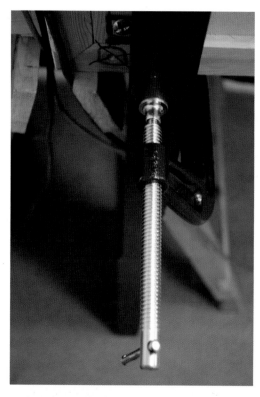

THIS PAGE:

LEFT: *The upright stanchion of the lighting frame, connected to the back-scene board frames using 'G' clamps.*

BELOW: *The whole layout ready for presentation, with the lighting rig assembled; in the early days, this layout lacked a back scene.*

OPPOSITE PAGE:

TOP LEFT: *A layout on show at the Stafford exhibition. The owner has opted to use tubular steel stanchions with spotlights fitted to the inside of the plywood pelmet.*

TOP RIGHT: *Another layout seen at the Stafford exhibition, with no lighting pelmet. Hiding the lighting behind a pelmet or facia valance does tend to give a more professional look.*

BOTTOM LEFT: *Another layout at the Stafford exhibition, using the same arrangement of lighting rig.*

BOTTOM RIGHT: *The Mickleover Model Railway Group's layout 'Farkham'. Viewed from the rear, the lighting frame is apparent. The construction is similar to that used for 'Eccleston', but the cross-bars to hold the lighting pelmet have a nice curve to them.*

ABOVE: *Fluorescent tubes have been used for 'Farkham', using the same style of cables and connecting plugs as those seen on 'Eccleston'.*

LEFT: *The lighting rig for 'Summit Colliery', on which Ian Mellors has used the modern option of LEDs on a ribbon. The ribbons can be joined together if a longer length is required.*

PRESENTATION

Once you have made all your lighting decisions, you need to finish off the layout by arranging precisely how it will be presented. This applies mainly to layouts and dioramas that will be on the exhibition circuit, although it may also be adapted to layouts situated at home. The smaller layouts and dioramas can be finished off by extending the frame from the valance on each side and across the base. This can be made with separate sections or as a one-piece frontage with a large aperture cut out, giving a window on to the layout inside. In many ways, this presentation resembles a stage frontage, know as a proscenium arch, and a good number of modellers use the approach. If the frame is painted in a dark colour, the viewer's attention will be focused directly on to the layout.

On an end-to-end layout, the fiddle yard will usually appear at one end, or sometimes both ends, of the layout. One popular way to hide this is by the use of sidings appearing on a section reserved on the front of the layout. This will be divided by using a back-scene panel positioned directly in front of the fiddle yard, which is positioned at the rear of the same section. The front could accommodate a series of sidings or a motive power depot, perhaps. Another favourite use is for a private industrial siding serving a brewery, gasworks, or a dairy; alternatively, the space could accommodate a quayside or canal wharf.

The fiddle yard can also be disguised at one or both ends by providing a screen board in front. This will keep the viewer's attention concentrated on the visual part of the layout and not allow it to be distracted by operations in the fiddle yard. The boards can be painted in the same colour as the surround to the layout. The board can also be utilized for display purposes, perhaps with the addition of archive photographs of a prototype, track plans or other visual information regarding the layout. This will all provide extra interest for the viewing public at exhibitions.

The Mickleover Model Railway Group's 7mm scale layout 'Warner Street', ready to face the visiting public just before the opening of the Derby 2015 exhibition held at The Midland Railway Round House. The layout looks very professional, with its back scene (commissioned from me) and lighting frame, and is finished with a pelmet, boxed-in traverser and colour-coordinated front drapes. GEOFF CLARK

Finishing off the presentation of layouts and dioramas also means looking at the space below the level of the model. Most exhibition layouts will be supported on a series of trestles; fixed layouts will be supported in the same way, or on something similar. This will always create a void between the floor and the base boards, which does not look attractive and needs addressing, particularly when displaying the layout at exhibitions. The most common and simple way of overcoming this is by pinning up a cloth drape. This will hang from the back of the front facia of the layout or diorama's base boards to finish just short of the floor level. Velcro strip could be used instead of pins, for a more professional finish.

*LEFT: **This compact layout is contained in a frame mounted around 5ft (150cm) from the floor. It looks rather like a Punch and Judy stall, with its cloth drapes.***

*BELOW: **A small diorama layout modelled by Chris Nevard, showing just how professional a small layout can look when presented at an exhibition. The framing and lighting concentrate the viewer's attention on the model, which is complemented by an excellent diffused photographic back scene.***

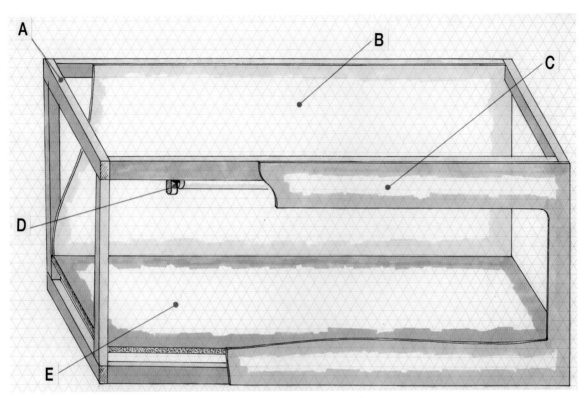

The construction of a small frame, which would be ideal for a small shunting layout or perhaps a small station in N-gauge. Such a layout is easily transportable in the average-sized family car for display at exhibitions, where it can either be supported on its own trestles or simply sit on a provided table top. A: the framework is made of 2 x 1in timber; B: a back-scene board fits inside the frame at the back. This might restrict space at the back, so operation from the front is advisable with this type of layout; C: the facia or pelmet extends down the sides to connect with the base-board facia, thus creating a total frame or proscenium arch for the diorama layout; D: one fluorescent tube provides the lighting; LED lighting would also be an option. The inside of the frame can be painted white to reflect all the light on to the layout. In contrast, the outside can be painted black or any other dark colour.

Smaller layouts and dioramas will always benefit from having a back scene presented on curved boards, excluding any awkward corners and right-angles appearing in the back scene. Although it will of course reduce the space available on the base board, it will definitely improve the overall visual appearance of the layout or diorama.

The depth of the back scene will depend on a few different factors, including the scale of the layout; it goes without saying that a 7mm-scale layout will require a deeper back scene than a 2mm-scale layout. If the layout is operated from the rear, then access will be needed for uncoupling or maintenance. This may become an issue if the back scene boards are too deep, particularly with exhibition layouts. As a result, some modellers take the decision to leave off the back scene completely, making the layout look totally unfinished. This is a shame, as it can easily be rectified, either by installing a low back scene or by opting to operate the layout from the front using hand-held controllers. The latter will allow for a reasonable depth of back scene to be fitted to finish off the layout.

Finally, you will need to consider the height of the layout base boards. The majority of layouts have the base boards set at only around 3ft (around 1m) from the floor. This will mean that most viewers will be looking down on both the layout and the back scene. A better solution would be to raise the base

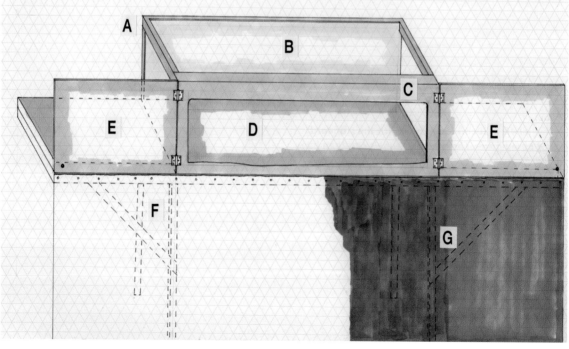

OPPOSITE PAGE:

TOP: 'Summit Colliery', presented at the 2016 Mansfield Model Railway Exhibition by its owner, Ian Mellors. The layout is complete with a photographic back scene and has a lighting rig of LED lighting strips mounted on to UPVC conduit panels which make up the pelmet. To complete the presentation a curtain is used to hide the supporting framework.

BOTTOM: Construction of a small layout diorama, designed to make the most of a small space when on display at exhibitions. This one can also be folded up even smaller for transit and storage. A: basic framework of the layout creating an open box construction; B: the back panel displaying the back scene; C: the facia frame or proscenium arch, with the aperture cut out to view the layout; D: the base board displaying the layout; E: the fold-out boards at each end hide the fiddle area and act as display panels for photographs, track plans and so on. The boards can fold back across the ends or the front when not in use, to protect the model; F: the legs have fold-out supports to connect with the fold-out base-board extensions to accommodate the fiddle arrangements; cassettes might be the best choice for this; G: cloth drapes are fixed to the front of the layout display, to hide the unsightly legs and any other clutter that might appear under or behind the layout. It all creates a professional-looking presentation.

THIS PAGE:

My preferred method for constructing a substantial back scene – for example, on 'Tawcombe' – is to use canvas-board panels. Canvas board gives a good white surface on which to paint the artwork, and is also easy to cut. This back scene depicts a panel made up from two standard 24 x 18in canvas boards, which are available from most art and craft stores. This makes up a panel 4ft (120cm) long, to fit with the standard sizes of base boards. The modular panels can then be easily bolted or screwed together to create any desired length. A: the framework is made from 2 x 1in timber, glued and screwed at the joints. The canvas boards can then be glued and pinned to the framework; B: for extra strength and rigidity, plywood or heavy-duty card triangular corner braces are glued and pinned in position on all four corners; C: a centre strut made from timber or plywood is then glued to the back of the canvas boards, bridging and supporting the join between the two boards. This joint must be made as tight as possible. Some white primer paint run along the joint on the facing side should create a flat textured surface, ready to take the painted artwork.

boards up to eye level from the ground, at around 5ft (150cm). This will give the viewer a more realistic impression of the three-dimensional model and the two-dimensional back scene beyond.

This will concentrate the viewpoint on to the railway and the trains passing by. Any land beyond the track bed can either fall away or rise towards the back scene. This can also fool the eye, to make the layout appear wider than it really is.

The only disadvantage of setting the base boards higher will become apparent at exhibitions, where younger viewers may not be able to see well. This can be easily rectified, however, by supplying a number of step-up boxes for children and the less tall among the audience, to gain the extra height. One enterprising modeller has even started to provide periscopes, to help those who are not so tall to view his layout at exhibitions.

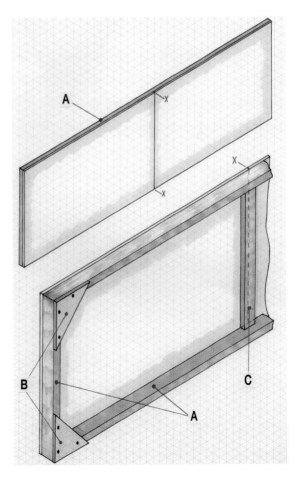

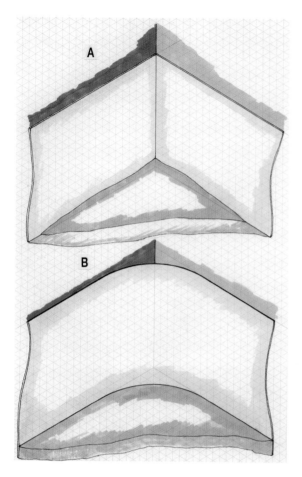

One other advantage of positioning the base boards higher is that it will be much easier for the operators to gain access. When the base boards are lower, the operators will often have to stoop down or even crawl underneath, which will inevitably become more of a problem with age. The problem of course applies only to continuous circuit layouts, and does not directly involve the back scene.

By putting all these elements together, and spending the extra time and money, you will be rewarded with a layout or model diorama you can be proud of, giving you and your visiting public, if you are presenting at exhibitions or yourself at home, many hours of enjoyment. Let's not forget when it comes to exhibiting our layouts or dioramas at the exhibitions we are all amateurs trying to give a professional presentation.

LEFT: *A right-angled corner (A) will benefit from being made curved (B). This way, the landscape will appear to continue around the corner without looking awkward.*

BELOW: *My first attempt at a model railway, showing how the back scene boards were painted and fixed into position before any landscaping was modelled on the base boards. It is always worth considering the back scene at an early stage and not leaving it as an afterthought.*

LEFT: *My first attempt again, this time the far right-hand side, with the scenery and bridge finished. The back scene was painted using acrylic paints on the rough side of 4 x 2 panels of hardboard. The colours used are almost completely monotone, focusing the viewer's attention on the train.*

RIGHT: *A number of problems may arise from positioning a layout too low to the ground. The best viewing point for models is at eye level, as in real life. This position is also an advantage for operators wishing to gain access to the rear of a full circuit layout, so it is worth taking this aspect into consideration if agility is an issue. The top 3D illustration shows a layout mounted around 5ft (150cm) from the ground (A). The track bed is elevated even higher, taking in the depth of the base board (B) and the risers holding the base for the track bed (Z), to reach eye level for viewing at (C). The width of the base boards (around 2ft/60cm) has also been included at this point (D). In the lower illustration, this has been repeated, to show the advantage of access under the base boards as well as a correct viewing point. This has all been indicated in red, with the clearance shown at (X). The section of the illustration reproduced in black indicates the disadvantage of setting the base boards too low to the ground, creating a very limited clearance at (X). The operator would have to crawl underneath to gain access to the rear.*

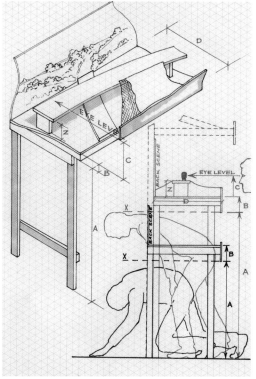

CHAPTER NINE

PORTFOLIO

There follows here a selection of images related to the back scene, using subject matter covered throughout the book, with a view to considering the positives and negatives of each layout. The layouts all include a back scene of some kind; any comments are not intended to criticize, but to explore how any problems might be avoided when planning and building a layout or diorama.

The selection also shows a few more prototype images, again with comments that have been made with a view to using the images either for reference or as direct subject matter for producing a back scene. Layout plans are also included, accompanied by three-dimensional illustrations, to give a good idea how the back scene relates to the layout in front.

Photographic back scene depicting a semi-rural colliery community, where the housing has spread out into the countryside. The ribbon housing would probably have housed miners and their families.

OPPOSITE PAGE:

TOP: *The industrial colliery landscape continues on the back scene with the inclusion of a conical pit-waste tip. This type of tip was a regular feature of the coal fields until the 1960s. This back scene works very well for this layout, although it could have been improved by diffusing slightly the hard edge produced from cutting out the photographic image and mounting it on to a plain sky.*

BOTTOM: *Softening the edges of the trees in the mid-ground and the hills on the skyline has improved this layout.*

OPPOSITE PAGE:

TOP: *A layout at the Stafford exhibition, showing how a building modelled in low relief with a flat roof can work well with the back scene. Here, the subject is a block of flats, which has unfortunately thrown a shadow on the back scene. This is sometimes unavoidable, but careful positioning of the lighting or diffusing the light source can alleviate the worst of any hard shadows.*

BOTTOM: *The same layout, showing more low-relief buildings blending well with the back scene. The weathering on the shop roofs is especially convincing, with the rain staining and the coating of green algae having been reproduced very well. Clearly, the modeller has observed the subject very carefully.*

A rural mountain scene, created using cut-out photographs pasted on to a painted sky. The hard edge created by using this method is difficult to rectify, but it might be softened by using an airbrush with a concentrated flow of light blue paint. The castle ruins on the hillside over the tunnel add rustic charm and blend in well with the back scene, perhaps because they have a broken edge to them rather than hard, straight lines.

'Stoney Lane Depot', a South London urban layout that features some super urban buildings modelled in full, half and low relief. Graham Hedges has successfully blended the three-dimensional urban model into the two-dimensional back scene, using a combination of low-relief model buildings, photographic cut-outs and sections of painted back scene. Careful attention has been paid to making sure the transition works from every angle. GRAHAM HEDGES

ABOVE: **A commercially available photographic back scene; depicting a rural landscape, it works well behind the prefabricated colliery screens on 'Summit Colliery'.**

LEFT: **'Summit Colliery's sorting screens, showing the back scene beyond.**

RIGHT: *The newly painted urban back scene created for the first exhibition of Mickleover Model Railway Group's 7mm layout 'Warner Street', at the Derby Roundhouse.*

BELOW: *The back scene of the 'Loughborough Midland' layout, on display at the East Midlands Nottingham exhibition. The scene is dominated by the 'Brush' engineering works immediately behind the station. The large complex of buildings and their industrial paraphernalia were photographed, cut out and pasted on to the skyscape, causing a number of issues. Just about all the verticals appear at conflicting angles. This is because the photographs were taken at ground level; perspective has made the walls on the tall structures appear to slope inwards. This might work if the model is viewed from the same viewpoint – eye level – but the railway and the station on the layout are viewed from above. Either the photographs need to be taken from a higher viewpoint, or they need to be downloaded on to a computer and corrected using software such as Photoshop. Both solutions will involve some planning. Alternatively, the structures could be drawn in and painted, but that would require a certain amount of confidence and draughting skills.*

OPPOSITE PAGE:

TOP: A tunnel and surrounding landscape can make the ideal scenic break for a layout. On this example, modeller John Gaskin has managed to create the depth of the rock cutting around the tunnel mouth. The model is based on Rise Hill on the Settle & Carlisle railway for the tunnel portal, with the surrounding rock cutting based on Headstone Tunnel on the Peak Line. The sculpted limestone cutting is probably deep enough that the layout does not necessarily need a back scene, although a little would complete it perfectly.

BOTTOM: In this prototype rural landscape, the sky, trees, hedgerows and farmstead all provide valuable reference material for producing this type of scene for a model railway.

A photograph of a hedgerow and gateway, useful reference for a rural back scene.

Another hedgerow, this time including a tree to use for reference.

A photograph taken out of a third-floor window in Mansfield. It is always worth keeping an eye open for scenes that might be useful. This urban composition, looking over the town's rooftops and dominated by the stone-arched railway viaduct, would make the ideal back scene for a small diorama. The scene could also be used as reference for part of a larger layout back scene.

When creating a back scene for a modern rural railway, it is worth considering the inclusion of a wind turbine, or indeed a whole farm. They may be controversial, but they are an unmissable part of the landscape today, as are solar farms and mobile-phone masts.

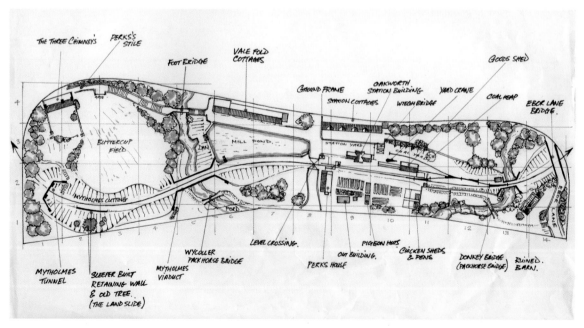

A track plan of a small layout that was drawn up for a model railway project based on the classic film **The Railway Children.**

Along with the flat plan, the three-dimensional interpretation shows the relationship between the model and the back scene. The 'Vale Cottages' row has been modelled in full, along with 'The Three Chimneys'. Because they are right at the back of the layout, they could, along with the surrounding features, be modelled in a slightly smaller scale. The cottages positioned immediately behind the station are modelled in low relief, with the roof line taken over the ridge. The cottages could also be taken down a size or forced perspective could be applied. The large mill, with its tall chimney, has been painted on the back scene with a tree line positioned at the base to help blend it into the three-dimensional modelling directly in front of it.

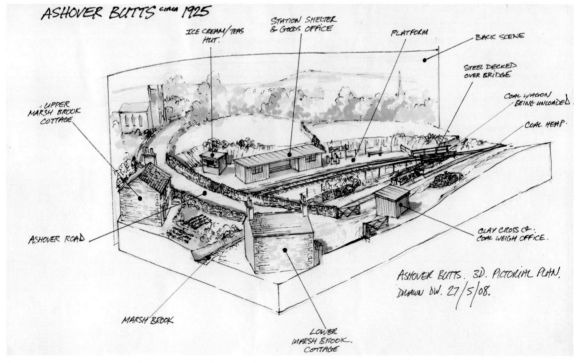

A three-dimensional sketch drawing of 'Ashover Butts', which was drawn to show how the road might appear, disappearing off the model and on to the two-dimensional back scene. By curving the road, the perspective works better and looks more convincing.

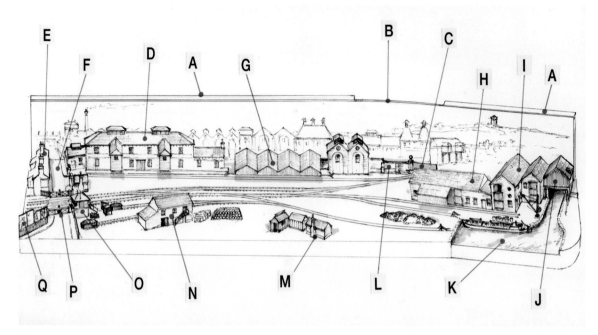

Illustration of an urban brewery branch line, based on the system once found in Burton-on-Trent, and showing how the urban scene relates to the backdrop. The plan also includes the canal wharf at Horninglow. A: the framework on the back of the base back scene boards is made in two sections, with one larger section to fit along the rear length of the layout, and the shorter frame to fit at the shallow angle; B: this part of the back scene board has a gentle curve at this point. I suggest using the 6mm flexible MDF board now available for this; C: one end of this section has an aperture cut into it at the base to create an exit for the trains to reach the fiddle yard; D: this large malthouse is built in low relief and fits up to the back scene boards. The roof line again is modelled over the ridge with the hipped roofed ventilators modelled in full; E: the terraced row of cottages, including the pub at the near end, is modelled using forced perspective; F: the street also follows the same perspective and is carried on in painted version on the back scene; G: along with the twin-gabled brewery buildings, the multiple canopy roofs protecting the ale dock are also modelled up to the back scene boards. The roof line of buildings running at right-angles to the back boards usually work better; H: this warehouse is modelled almost in full with the rear wall fitting up to the angled section of the back scene boards; I: the two warehouses here are at right-angles to the angled back scene board; J: the final building along this section is the salt warehouse, which again runs at right angles to the back scene board. This building as you can see also accommodates the main line of the canal as it runs into the wharf; K: the wharf or canal basin complete with a narrow boat; L: a section of perimeter wall runs up to the back scene boards and also helps towards masking the join; M: the coal merchant's offices fit into the foreground of the layout; N: another brewery building to accommodate on this model would be the cooperage; O: most of the brewery branches in Burton-on-Trent were part of the Midland Railway featuring the company's signals and signal boxes. Here a typical box has been used to control the points and the crossing gates: P: the crossing gates are also of the familiar Midland pattern; Q: at this end of the layout advertising hoardings have been used to mask and create the scenic break. This type of hoarding was a common feature found near to the railway crossings, possibly advertising the many beers brewed in the town.

This delightful archive image of Bass No. 10 on a REC Special was taken back in September 1961. The unique wedge-shaped signal box is of special interest, the perfect example of how to model half- and low-relief buildings in a very restricted area. The box stood at High Street Crossing in Burton-on-Trent and was only the width of the door at one end, and half the width of a standard signal box at the road end. This resulted in the hipped roof being cut off vertical at the back, with the ridge sloping from one end to the other. How much room was there for the signal man, alongside the lever frame, gate operating wheel and stove? Generally, half-relief model buildings should not be cut along the ridge when fitting up against the back scene, but this proyotype shows that the rules do not always apply! TREVOR OWEN/COLOUR RAIL

LIST OF
SUPPLIERS

HARDBOARD, MDF AND PLYWOOD

B&Q DIY Supplies and Accessories (diy.com)
Homebase DIY (homebase.co.uk)
Jewson Timber Merchants (jewson.co.uk/timber)
Wickes (Tel: 0330 123 4123; Wickes.co.uk)

BASE BOARDS AND DIORAMA KITS

Tim Horn
Precision Scale Replicas and Layout Accessories
9c Millers Close, Fakenham, Norfolk NR21 8NW
Tel: 07920 510 890
timhorn.co.uk

CANVAS ROLL
AND CANVAS BOARD

Winsor & Newton
winsornewton.com
Daler Rowney Limited
PO Box 10, Bracknell,
Berks RG12 4ST
Tel: 01344 424621
Picture Master Co. Ltd
Unit 8, Rea Business Park, Inkerman Street,
Birmingham B7 4SH
Tel: 0870 9777 987
The Range
Wellington Street, Burton-on-Trent, Staffordshire
DE4 2AP
tiendeo.co.uk
Hobbycraft
hobbycraft.co.uk

ACRYLIC SPRAY PAINTS

Halfords
Tel: 0345 5045353
halfords.com

ACRYLICS, WATERCOLOUR
AND OIL PAINTS

The Range
Winsor & Newton
Daler Rowney Limited

GENERAL PAINTBRUSHES

Wicks
B&Q DIY Supplies and Accessories (diy.com)
Homebase DIY
homebase.co.uk
Wilkos Artist range of brushes
Rosemary & Co.
PO Box 372, Keighley, West Yorkshire BD20 6WZ
Tel: 01535 600090
rosemaryandco.com
Frank Herring & Sons
27 High Street, Dorchester, Dorset DT1 1UP
Tel: 01305 264449/267917
Hobbycraft
Winsor & Newton
Daler Rowney Limited
The Range

SOFTWARE SUPPLIERS

Adobe Photoshop
photoshop.com/products
adobe-student.com

PRINTING

John E Wright Limited
Blue Print House, 115 Huntingdon Street,
Nottingham NG1 3NF
Tel: 0115 950 6633
15 Brick Street, Derby DE1 1DU
Tel: 01332 244743

TREES, BUSHES, GRASS AND UNDERGROWTH
The Model Tree Shop
4 David Hume View, Chirnside, Duns TD11 3SX
Tel: 01890 819021
themodeltreeshop.co.uk
Hedgerow Scenics
Rob Spedelow
25 Kensington Close, Lower Earley, Reading RG6 4EY
Tel: 01189 867020
hedgerowscenics.co.uk
Green Scene
60 Hollymount, Worcester WR4 9SF
Tel: 01905 24298
http//green-scene.co.uk
Woodland Scenics
PO Box 98, Linn Creek, MO 65052, USA
Tel: 573-346-5555
woodlandscenics.com
HEKI Kittler GmbH
Am Bahndamm 10. D-76437 Rastatt-Wintersdord, Germany
Tel: 07229 18 17 15
heki-kittler.de

GLUES, ADHESIVES AND SPECIAL EFFECTS
Deluxe Materials Ltd
Unit 13, Cufaude Business Park, Bramley, Hampshire RG26 5DL
Tel: 01256 883944
deluxematerials.com

PLASTER/PLASTER BANDAGE
Gaugemaster
Gaugemaster House, Ford Road, Arundel, West Sussex BN18 0BN
gaugemaster.com

LOW-RELIEF BUILDINGS AND KITS
Bachmann Scenecraft
bachmann.co.uk

Skytrex 2013
Unit 1A Charnwood Business Park, North Road, Loughborough, Leicestershire LE11 1LE
Tel: 01509 213789
skystrex.com

TUBES AND LEDS
Maplin Electronics
Tel: 0333 400 9500

FLUORESCENT LIGHTING
philips.co.uk/fluorescent-lighting
W.T. Lighting
150 Uttoxeter Road, Longton, Stoke-on-Trent, Staffordshire ST3 1PX
Tel: 01782 319743
wtlighting.co.uk
Wickes

CABLES, WIRING AND PLUGS
Maplin Electronics

PRESENTATION
Velcro strip or fabric fasteners
velcro.co.uk/products/forfabrics

BESPOKE BASE BOARDS AND DIORAMA FRAMES
Tim Horn
9c Millers Close, Fakenham, Norfolk NR21 8NW
Tel: 07920 510 890
timhorn.co.uk

BESPOKE BACK SCENE PAINTING SERVICE
Dovedale Models
David Wright – Back Scene Services
6 Ivy Court, Hilton, Derbyshire DE65 5WD
Tel: 01283 733547
dovedalemodels.co.uk

CUSTOM DIGITAL IMAGES AND PRINTING
Clive Baker – Technical Illustrator
66 Meadow View, Rolleston, Burton-on-Trent, Staffordshire DE13 9AN
Tel: 01283 815115
clive-baker.co.uk

BOOKS
Layout Design, by Ian Rice (Haynes Publishing, Sparkford, Yeovil, Somerset BA22 7JJ)
Tel: 01963 442030
haynes.co.uk

DVDS AND MODEL-MAKING WORKSHOPS
Painting the Back Scene and Making Model Trees (for the miniature landscape), by David Wright (Dovedale Models, 6 Ivy Court, Hilton, Derbyshire DE65 5WD; Tel: 01283 733547; dovedalemodels.co.uk)

ONLINE ARCHIVE SERVICES
Picture the Past
picturethepast.org.uk
Colour Rail
558 Birmingham Road, Bromsgrove, Worcestershire B61 0HT
Tel: 0121 453 6518
colourrail.com

INDEX

RELATED TITLES FROM CROWOOD

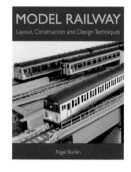
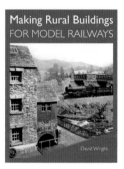
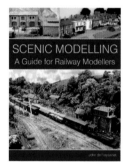
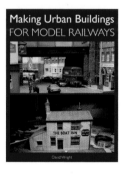